The
CAPTAIN'S
Diary

**ENGLAND IN FIJI, NEW ZEALAND AND PAKISTAN
1983–84**

The CAPTAIN'S *Diary*

ENGLAND IN FIJI, NEW ZEALAND AND PAKISTAN 1983–84

IN CONJUNCTION WITH
ALAN LEE

Photographs by
ADRIAN MURRELL

WILLOW BOOKS
Collins
8 Grafton Street, London W1
1984

Willow Books
William Collins Sons & Co Ltd
London · Glasgow · Sydney · Auckland
Toronto · Johannesburg

First published 1984

© Bob Willis and Alan Lee 1984
New Zealand Scorecards © Bill Frindall 1984

Willis, Bob
    The captain's diary.
    1. Test matches (Cricket)—England
    I. Title
    796.35'865   GV923
ISBN 0-00-218115-0

All photography bv Adrian Murrell/All-Sport
unless otherwise specified

Set in Monophoto Plantin
by Ace Filmsetting Ltd, Frome, Somerset
Printed in Great Britain

CONTENTS

FOREWORD
BY GEOFF HOWARTH

Time flies. It is now fully fifteen years since I first arrived at The Oval and set eyes on the gangling, bushy-haired young fast bowler who was to become one of my closest mates. We have both come a long way since then.

Being almost two years older than the novice Kiwi, Robert George Dylan rather took me under his wing as we both tried to make our way in the Surrey ranks that long ago summer. We got along pretty well, discovered we had largely the same tastes and sense of humour, and as I had to spend a full year in England to complete residential qualifications, Bob offered me the spare room in the house at Stoke d'Abernon where he was living with his parents.

Little did either of us imagine during those frivolous, fanciful days that the time would come when we would find ourselves walking out together on some of the world's greatest cricket grounds as captains of England and New Zealand. But that is how things worked out and, in the space of twelve recent months, we were in opposition in seven Tests and no less than thirteen one-day internationals. Twenty times, Bob and I performed the pre-match toss, swapped a few yarns and, more than once, reminisced just a bit.

Bob's bowling has altered a great deal since I first knew him. He used to be extremely fast and more than a little erratic. Three or four balls out of six had a very good chance of going down the leg-side as he strained for that extra inch of speed. He was a shock weapon, and could be very effective. But he could also be very expensive. Over the past few years his bowling has matured in wisdom and consistency to such a degree that when we in the New Zealand side discuss facing him, the common complaint is that he gives the batsman no room to play shots. His line is so constantly accurate that, these days, hardly a single delivery strays down the legside. I don't .think he will mind me saying he never had great natural talent, because this is far from being an insult, much more a compliment to the quite staggering pride of performance which has driven him to work so hard at his game and overcome a whole series of setbacks. He is one of cricket's greatest competitors, yet he has never sacrificed the personality I find so endearing.

I doubt whether two opposing Test captains have ever been as close, off the field, as Bob and myself. It certainly never makes us want to win any the less – probably quite the opposite, in fact – but I happen to believe it has helped foster a healthy, friendly relationship between the players of England and New Zealand. Bob and I might differ in our interpretation of an incident, we might find different things to grieve us in a day's play but, so far at least, we have always been on speaking terms at the end of each day. I think our friendship has spread to other players in our teams.

There was a fine spirit between the teams during the summer of 1983, the four-match series won three–one by England. I ended that rubber with very mixed feelings because, although I had led New Zealand to a first-ever Test win in England, I could not help thinking we had let ourselves down in the final two games and allowed England to take the series by a flattering margin. I was delighted to have an early opportunity to put things right; delighted, too, that what little success we had achieved had created an astonishing upsurge of public interest in the game all around New Zealand. It might have added extra strain to my job, through the unusual pressure of being expected to produce the goods by an ever-expanding public, but I could easily put up with that for the pleasure of being followed by huge crowds wherever we appeared.

After the first two days of the winter series my confidence had been dented, and it looked as if England might finish us off with a day to spare. But we proved we had the ability to fight back, and the escape injected us with renewed conviction, which we carried through the series. Our win at Christchurch was enough, and although it was certainly not achieved on the best of Test pitches, I believe England allowed themselves to be psyched out of contention by fears of how badly it might play.

It was a happy series and a memorable one for me, and at the parting of the ways in February, England flew on to face the rigours of Pakistan while we in the New Zealand team set off for humid Sri Lanka. The merry-go-round continued on its way, but I was certain of one thing. Come May, and the new season, Bob and I would be meeting up again, and nothing would have changed.

1

ELEVENTH
TIME AROUND

Eleventh time around, and the routine is like an old friend now: comfortably familiar, not the awesome test of nerves it once seemed. I could recite the day's timetable by heart, account for virtually every minute. Little changes. But then that is how it should be on this traditional eve-of-tour gathering – a gentle indoctrination for the nervous new boys, a chance to dispose of mundane essentials before the sterner business begins. It is an exciting day due only to anticipation; the actual events are marked by the predictable and the pedantic.

Some things are different this year, though. We are setting off later than usual, after the rare luxury of a Christmas at home. We are heading, by way of a brief stop in Fiji, for New Zealand to play our first Tests, another departure from tradition. We have only fifteen players instead of the customary sixteen, only one wicket-keeper rather than two. But there the contradictions end. We are gathered, sporting new team blazers, new haircuts and no doubt some new ideas. It has been like this every year since I first won an England cap thirteen years ago, and I doubt if the syndrome will change much in the next thirteen years either.

It seems a long time ago, that first tour I made to Australia. I am thirty-four now, going on thirty-five, and, for all the smug satisfaction I have often felt at reviving my career when many considered it finished, there is now no escaping the fact that I do not have long left at this level. There is only a certain amount the human body can achieve against the odds of nature and I don't kid myself that I am markedly more like Peter Pan than the next man.

The thought has troubled me increasingly over the past six months: not the fear of physically divorcing myself from playing the game (when I know the time is right I somehow doubt if I will find that too hard), more the uncertainty of what lies beyond retirement. A cricketer's life is short, unless you happen to be of the mind and resilience of Jack Hobbs, Bill Alley or Ray Illingworth and

9

cheat the pension book into your fifties. I am not made that way, physically or mentally. When I can no longer bowl fast my value to a side will dimish so dramatically that I will pack up, not waiting for what to me would be the agonisingly slow death of lingering too long in county cricket.

More than once in recent months I have thought hard about quitting, especially, of course, when things have got rough. But up to now there has always been a silver lining somewhere to keep me going. It won't always be that way and I am increasingly conscious of a desire to get out of the game while I am still on top, fighting a sub-conscious battle with my wish to go on playing for England as long as I am capable.

I am glad to have got this far, to stand on the threshold of yet another tour. Words like 'honour' and 'privilege' sound fairly hackneyed, but they still sum up my pride in playing for my country, not to mention captaining it. The job came as a surprise, as I have stressed many times before, and there have been times when it has hung like a lead weight round my neck. Even before I was put in charge, I was always one to take the team's performance to heart; now that I am at least partly responsible for failure, my moods and emotions reflect still more sharply the fortunes of my team-mates. It is not always a good thing to be so deeply involved. I realize now just how much it alters my entire personality. During the English season, and particularly around Test time, I confess to being poor company – uncommunicative, sometimes to the point of surliness. Out of season, and away from touring months, I am a different person. I felt the 'change' more acutely than ever this year. In September it was as if I shed one costume for another, and autumn passed in a pleasurable, sociable mood which those who encounter me in mid-summer might find it difficult to believe I possess.

In a sense, I suppose I am constantly torturing myself by mentally reliving every moment of every Test. But I have reached this point of my life knowing that Test cricket is the thing I do best, and I only know one way to approach it. If it sometimes offends those on the outside, I am sorry. But I doubt if I will change.

This past summer was an important one for English cricket and, having retained the captaincy following the loss of the Ashes in Australia, I was inevitably the man in the spotlight as we began a demanding schedule taking in the World Cup tournament prior to a four-match Cornhill Test series against New Zealand.

There are a number of traits common to the sporting public of Britain which I will touch on, the first of them being an almost indecent haste to cry for the sacking of established players and officials at the first sign of a setback. But being a shade long in the tooth can be an advantage – I was ready for it, well aware that there were many who thought I should be replaced as captain and some who went so far as to insist I was no longer worth my place as a bowler.

By the end of the summer, I believe I had done much to answer both charges. Certainly, there seemed little speculation in the press, nor with the public within my earshot, about my being made captain for this winter tour, while my own satisfying season with the ball, allied to persisting doubts regarding the speed, skill or staying-power of various other pace-bowling candidates, smoothed my re-election in that department.

It could be argued that neither circumstance is a sign of the English game being in robust health. Why are there no younger captains pressing me harder for the job? Why do we still find it so difficult to produce fast bowlers that a man in his mid-thirties automatically takes the new ball? The answers to these questions, and the arguments surrounding them, have filled many an article before now, but suffice it to say I did not reach this new tour in a state of depression about our game. Far from it. I am, overall, happier with the strength of the English squad than I was before we left for Australia last year; and, if we can continue to build patiently, I feel there are indications that we could have a side of some substance in a year or two.

Such optimism from a natural pessimist would probably have seemed out of place when England, having returned from the Antipodes with a defeat in the Test series and an embarrassment in the limited-overs games which followed, then proceeded to lose to India in the semi-final of Prudential's World Cup in June. Yet, although that defeat was a surprise and a disappointment, I did not regard it as a disaster, nor as the signal for renewed outbursts of 'sack the lot' hysteria. For one thing, India went on to create a far bigger shock by beating the West Indies to win the trophy; for another, we had played with such competence and confidence for most of the qualifying stages that the competition seemed, in my view, to have produced more good points than bad.

There was criticism throughout over our preference for Mike

Gatting ahead of Derek Randall, but few seemed to appreciate Gatting's value was as the stand-by bowler: without him, we would have been taking an enormous risk for, apart from the five chosen bowlers, there would have been no one else capable of giving even a passable impression. If Graham Dilley or I had pulled a muscle in the first over and taken no further part, we would have had to make do with the terrifying seamers of Chris Tavaré or the tempting off-spin of David Gower – not a comforting thought.

Having said that, the selected side did all that could have been asked of them. Apart from one disturbing show of overconfident batting which cost us dear against New Zealand at Edgbaston, we were convincing winners of all our group games, twice beating the Pakistanis, whose short odds for the cup were mystifying to me.

The semi-final pitch at Old Trafford was very disappointing for a one-day match. One cannot blame the groundsman – he is simply suffering the legacy of his predecessors and finds himself forced to turn out wickets like this, on which the slower one bowled the ball, the more difficult it was to hit. Mohinder Amarnath and Kirti Azad, Indian seamers so medium in pace that they are unkindly known as 'trundlers' or 'dobbers', were the incongruous match-winners as our opponents adapted to the conditions more readily than we did.

I had expected, deep down, to reach the final and then probably be beaten by the West Indies. But I was far from downhearted at the end of a sunny, glamorous event which might only have been improved by an initial round-robin qualifying series rather than the split into two groups. It did not seem right to me that we reached the semi-final of a World Cup yet went out without playing either Australia or the West Indies.

The tournament proved once again that we do not have sufficient competition for England places. Despite the modest success-rate of the previous winter's touring party, almost all of its members came home knowing they were still likely to play Tests and one-day internationals in the summer because they remained the best players in the country. This bred a natural complacency, sub-conscious or not, and I found it disturbing to see how readily many of the blokes accepted a poor performance or a bad result, and how quickly they resigned themselves to defeat and forgot about it. This, too, I believe, is an English trait and one which I can find little to commend. Pride in performance is essential in a successful team.

I emerged from the World Cup with the same conclusion I had brought home from New Zealand a few short months earlier. We must get harder; we must show we are hungry to win and drop the gentlemanly English attitude of doing just enough to win and being reluctant to grind the opposition into the dust.

It was satisfying to be able to introduce some new blood during the Cornhill series which followed the World Cup. Chris Smith, Nick Cook and Neil Foster all made Test débuts and did well enough to command places on the tour. Cook's performance was staggering: called up on the eve of the Lord's Test when Phil Edmonds 'went lame', he proceeded to take seventeen wickets in two games, bowling and conducting himself with a maturity beyond his experience. Oddly, apart from in one second-team match some years ago, I had never played with or against Nick, nor met him socially, until we came together at Lord's. It did not take him long to impress me.

New Zealand are no longer the whipping boys they once were but, in all honesty, it would have been a depressing reflection on the standard of our game if we had not administered a convincing beating on our own pitches. The public, too, seemed to have that in mind and largely ignored the opening match of the series at The Oval. There were other factors involved, amongst them a natural hangover from such a surfeit of exciting cricket during the World Cup, and the almost intolerably hot spell which made south London a distinctly unappealing furnace. But I could not help feeling this lack of enthusiasm was an example of another familiarly English attitude, a rebellion against easy victories. In the main, English cricket-lovers would prefer to see their team narrowly beaten by a good side than witness the demolition of poor opponents. Crowds here appreciate the opposition, more so than anywhere else in the cricket world, and they want to see an even contest no matter who wins. On the occasions when England score overwhelming victories, the tendency is to demean the opposition as 'useless' rather than enthuse over the win. In my experience this attitude is unique and, while it is undoubtedly healthy and sporting, it is not always easy for the English players concerned to see it in that light.

Fortunately for the public and the series, if not for us, our big win at The Oval was negated in the next match when New Zealand's historic win levelled things up and ensured a huge upsurge in interest for the remaining two matches. Their first Test win in

England was fully merited but the pitch on which it occurred was commonly agreed to be sub-standard. Test wickets should be good and true nine times out of ten, but in recent years Headingley have not succeeded in coming anywhere near that number. Their pitch has been unacceptably poor on several recent occasions, but this was probably the worst. It was a case of 'hunt the ball', and New Zealand succeeded in finding it more often than we did. The Melbourne ground went through a similar period of producing one bad pitch after another. Eventually, years too late, they summoned the courage to dig up the square and relay it. Those measures are now overdue at Leeds and I hope current efforts there will put it right.

Lord's, venue of the Third Test, was not a great deal better, but we had a little bit of good fortune and eventually won convincingly, with Cook playing the starring role. Nottingham staged the final game, and on the easiest pitch of the lot we murdered New Zealand to take the series three–one.

By the end of the summer I was far happier with my captaincy than I had been twelve or even six months earlier. I feel confident now about the five-day job, although sometimes in limited-overs games I am still not totally assured when it comes to deviating from a set pattern. In Australia last winter the one-day games were an undermining experience for me: perhaps some of the criticisms directed at my leadership had some merit. I may well be more stereotyped in my thinking than some, and the fact that I have to concentrate on my own bowling as well does have some bearing on this. But if I am not the most adventurous tactician, it could be that I happen to consider it equally important, if not more so, to instil a pride and passion in the players under me. There are many more ways of doing that than by changing the bowling.

A new element has crept into the duties of Test captains in recent times, namely the need to dictate to players the balance between doing their job and making money. The two may seem synonymous, but that is not necessarily so. Consider the hypothetical case of a young and potentially exciting player starting out in Test cricket surrounded by a buzz of publicity. As if the newspapers were not enough to turn his head, he is quite likely to find himself offered substantial sums of money to appear in a TV commercial, open a sports shop or speak at dinners. He has to remember that the tail cannot wag the dog. The money is tempting, but will disappear quickly if he stops performing on the park and loses his Test place.

It is particularly hard for the guys to keep this in mind when they are asked to do something mundane, such as catching practice. It is all too easy for the mind to wander towards the £1000 an hour they could be earning elsewhere, disregarding the logical need to practise in order to stay at the top and retain the outlets for financial gain.

Soccer has this problem in a far more advanced stage than cricket. In the twelve months before the start of this tour, I saw no more than half-a-dozen matches live but found myself struck by the number of First Division players who could not kick with both feet, could not trap the ball and could not shoot straight more than once out of five attempts. All of them, no doubt, were on incredibly inflated contracts – £50,000 a year, it seems, is barely enough these days – and many, I am sure, had fallen foul of the tendency to let their superstar status rule their head and deflect them from the actual business of playing the game.

There is a worrying danger of cricket going the same way. Players whose egos have grown faster than their average can slip into the attitude that anything which does not produce any cash is not worth bothering with. But in sport there are many things which the player will not directly be paid for which must be done and, just as important for the public image, must be seen to be done.

Everyone goes through the immature stage of considering certain things beneath concern but cricket history shows that those who work hardest at the unglamorous sides of the game are those with the most enduring success stories. I found out in time how important it was to me to train properly; had I not got the message and acted on it, I would not have been around to knock out Jeff Crowe's middle stump at Headingley for my 300th Test wicket in July.

I ended the summer with 305, two short of the English all-time record held by F. S. Trueman. People were forever asking what it meant to me so I find it necessary to explain that I always have great difficulty in savouring the great moments. It was the same at Leeds two years earlier, when I took eight for 43 in the win over Australia. The euphoria of the occasion was lost on me. So, although it was a thrill to dismiss Crowe that day, and join an elite band of men, I did not stay awake all night gloating over it.

I doubt somehow if 300 wickets will be achieved many more times. Ian Botham should do it easily, and I fancy Malcolm Marshall has the skill and the stamina for it, but Test players' careers are contracting as the cricket calendar becomes ever more cluttered. It will not be easy for any newcomer to stay the course. I look, for instance, at the three young fast bowlers in our tour party – Graham Dilley, Norman Cowans and Neil Foster. Dilley is the most experienced, with seventeen Tests, while the other two are only just starting out. My own Test career is already thirteen-years old but, without any reflection on their stamina or character, I cannot believe any of the three will survive that long in the current cricketing climate.

The microscope will be on all three of them in the months ahead, although I do hope that not too much will be expected of Foster. He is not a very quick bowler but he has a tremendous action and gets very close to the stumps. His line and length have been exemplary when I have seen him and, as a long-term prospect, one worries only about his ability to overcome totally the back complaint which has required two operations. For this tour, however, his selection was a risk through his obvious inexperience and I will not be looking for him to make headlines.

It is in his department that we have been so bereft of choice since the exodus to South Africa, and the subsequent suspensions. People tend to think of Graham Gooch as the man we have missed most, and I would be the first to acknowledge that we would have been a better side, these past two years, with him opening the innings. But it is in the seam-bowling section that we have been left shortest since losing Chris Old, Mike Hendrick and the terribly under-rated John Lever, any one of whom would have been invaluable.

Dilley has something to prove on tour. He has shown a commendable improvement in attitude and deserves another chance but he, like Cowans, must now convince us he can take wickets consistently at the highest level.

This particular touring party actually took less selecting than most. The options were not large and there were never likely to be many surprises. Most comment was aroused by the decision to take only one wicket-keeper and reduce the party's strength to fifteen. While accepting the slim possibility that we could be left in the lurch if Bob Taylor happens to break a finger on the morning of a Test, I feel it would have been soul-destroying for any second-string keeper in an itinerary which would probably have permitted him no more than four days of cricket all tour. The same would have applied to a third spin bowler and, in the circumstances, it was thought better to take an extra batsman on the premise that two are always liable to fail on a tour, and that it is easier to keep spare batsmen match-fit than spare bowlers.

Mike Gatting might be said to have profited from the latter decision. He may well have been in the party anyway, but both he and Chris Smith must have believed their tour places were in doubt when their Trent Bridge failures burst the bubbles they had both done so much to blow up at Lord's. Gatting makes stacks of runs for Middlesex but has yet to make a century for England, which is simply not good enough. He will inevitably feel himself under pressure on this trip, but I would like to think he will make that maiden hundred and come out of the tour with an average of 45. Then he could go on to much better things.

Vic Marks, chosen to share the spin work with Cook, must disprove the general complaint that he is purely a one-day bowler. The usual outcry accompanied Phil Edmonds's omission from the party but the fact remains that Marks outbowled Edmonds when they played together in the Oval Test. Vic has a splendid temperament and is an ideal tourist, but he has been on the scene a fair while now and we must be looking for stronger indications that he can dismiss Test batsmen consistently.

Marks's phlegmatic nature will, however, be a bonus on this trip. Such are the contrasts of the countries we must visit, and the inconveniences we will certainly encounter in Pakistan, that the personality, patience and humour of each player will be tested to the full. Men like 'Skid' will hopefully help the younger and less experienced among us who may begin to fret at certain things.

We are all particularly anxious to visit New Zealand first despite the tradition of tagging it on to the end of a tour. Our schedule does not allow for many warm-up games, nor a great deal of acclimatization, but it will be preferable and more beneficial to spend the early weeks in New Zealand rather than in the limiting and slightly forbidding atmosphere of Pakistan.

Having toured New Zealand three times as a player, and visited it socially, I enjoy the place. It does not have the social vibrancy of Australia and one certainly can't walk down a main street after ten at night and expect to find a choice of places to eat and drink. But the people are friendly, the climate pleasant and the cricket much more competitive and taxing there than it used to be.

When I first went to New Zealand, at the end of the 1970–71

Australian tour, the England party was exhausted after what turned into a seven-Test Ashes series, and the last thing we really wanted was another few weeks of cricket against fresh opposition. To my knowledge this was the last occasion on which England handed out 'charity' caps for unlucky tourists – Bob Taylor and Don Wilson both being given a game on sentiment rather than merit.

The twin-tour idea is better for everyone concerned and the 1977–78 series there had much to commend it, despite well-chronicled troubles involving Geoff Boycott. New Zealand scored their first win over us, pointing the way ahead for a side that could no longer be taken lightly.

Last winter they humiliated our weary side in three one-day internationals, all played before full-house crowds – something which would have been unthinkable previously. The Australian format of one-day matches has certainly caught on in New Zealand and I only hope the public interest in instant cricket will be translated to the Tests this year.

Their side still tends to rely rather heavily on certain individuals. On good pitches, for instance, their bowling attack revolves almost exclusively around Richard Hadlee; the others are tremendous triers with only limited ability. The batting also lacks strength in depth. I consider John Wright to be their best player, the reluctant Glenn Turner apart, and other than Martin Crowe, who has a look of class about him, the middle-order is hardly formidable. Men like Jeremy Coney, however, have given substance to the team. Coney is under-rated – a workmanlike and very effective all-round cricketer – and I have no doubt he will have a big say in the series to come.

The success of the second half of the tour depends, too much for comfort, on the success of the first. If we have problems in New Zealand, if we are beaten in the three-Test series, then raising the lads' spirits for a not very popular month in Pakistan will not be an easy task. If, however, we sail through New Zealand and come away with the right result, morale will naturally be high enough to cope with the peculiar problems of this country.

Few cricketers, it has to be said, positively look forward to visiting Pakistan. Their political, religious and social customs can all be un-nerving to western Europeans and the natural response of an English sportsman is to laugh. But you can't do that in public in Pakistan.

Of our fifteen-man squad, only Taylor, Botham, Gatting and myself have made England tours there before and the newcomers will discover that time can apparently stand still when you finish play at 4.30 p.m. and have all evening to get through in the hotel. When I was younger, the thought of sitting in my room reading a book every night, eating bland food in the only hotel restaurant and not even being able to go out for a drink was appalling. I may have grown used to it, but I am sure some will struggle to adapt.

Illness is another hazard one has to accept there. People at home cannot possibly appreciate what it means to play sport when you are really ill. The condition which afflicts most in Pakistan is not like flu, or the sort of mild stomach upset one might get after eating a curry at home. Anyone with a bit of spirit can play cricket through such discomforts. In Pakistan I have known one or two who have felt they were going to die. I cite the case of Ian Botham, whom most of us consider indestructible. I have seen him get up and play a Test match in Australia the morning after a sleepless night vomiting caused by bad oysters. But in Pakistan six years ago he was defeated. He was so ill that, when by his request we organized a fitness test for him, he made ten yards out of the dressing-room and then collapsed.

If we can get through such things and keep our spirits high all will be well. Pitch conditions are, of course, another concern but at this distance I am more worried about the wickets in New Zealand, which are invariably poor, than those in Pakistan. The key here could be Imran Khan. If he is not fit to bowl, I can envisage us playing on three dead, flat pitches on which the Pakistan run-machines will be fancied to pile up runs by the hundred. If Imran is fit, the pitches will be livelier and we will have a more attractive series. We just might lose it, but it gives us a chance of winning, too.

I am convinced we are a better side than New Zealand. I feel we proved it last summer and now, in their back yard, we must prove it again. Pakistan are an entirely different proposition – a host of richly talented batsmen, one superb pace bowler if fit, and the help of conditions more familiar to them than to us. If we can win that series, it will be an achievement which says something for the growing strength of English cricket, and a lot more for the character of the men we are taking with us. It is character, above all else, that we will need to call upon to succeed on this tour.

2

THE CALM
BEFORE THE STORM

WEDNESDAY 28 DECEMBER In the current cluttered calendar of
international cricket one year can roll all too easily into the next –
another month, another series. This thought was hammered home
to me by a glance at last year's diary. On 28 December, it reminds
me, 'I had a violent attack of the trots'. More to the point, it des-
cribes day three of the Melbourne Test, which was one of the best,
most draining games in which I have played. It seems so long ago
somehow . . . so much has happened since. Now here we are again,
gathered for the time-honoured rituals of pre-departure day.

This year we have deserted Lord's indoor school, our regular
meeting place, for a suite in the Westmoreland hotel opposite. We
stay here whenever we play in London nowadays, so the territory
today was as familiar as the agenda. I arrived at 2.30 p.m. in order
to deal with any preliminary matters before the bulk of the party
turned up, an hour or so later. At 4.30 p.m. we posed like male
models for the pictures required by our various uniform sponsors,
Burtons, Kent & Curwens and Cheaneys. I then dealt with the
interviews for press, radio and television and at 6 p.m. we held a
brief team meeting to outline arrangements for tomorrow.

The last of the official engagements was the pre-tour dinner,
held in the Denis Compton suite and attended by various past
captains of tours to New Zealand and Pakistan, along with certain
high-ranking officials of the Test and County Cricket Board. I sat
between George Mann, who falls into the latter category, and Cecil
Burroughs, chairman of the Cornhill group which has now been
our Test sponsor for six years.

By 10 p.m. we had all downed the roast beef and toasted the
success of the tour, doubtless wondering a hundred times about the
treats and traumas in store for us over the next three months. I
retired to my room and my wife Juliet, who is expecting our first
child while I am away. We watched a Marx brothers film, the one
about the college football team. It wasn't memorable, but it filled

in time on a night of the year which always seems to drag unsatis-factorily. We are like sprinters poised on the starting blocks, primed for the race and chafed at the delay.

THURSDAY 29 DECEMBER/FRIDAY 30 DECEMBER Two days merged into one and as the final day of the year dawned we were still in the air en route to our acclimatizing and flag-waving stop-over in Fiji. Inevitably, the journey has not been without its incidents . . .

I missed breakfast in anticipation of a barrage of aircraft food and, after spending half an hour with Juliet making sure she had everything she needed, boarded our coach bound for Gatwick. The memories flooded back as we passed The Oval, then headed down the A23 through Brixton and Streatham Hill, where I had shared a flat in my Surrey days.

It was at the check-in counter for our Air New Zealand flight that the first minor irritation of the tour befell us. In previous years we have usually managed to reserve the six seats at the front of economy class for the taller members of our party (myself included) as they have unlimited legroom. Not so this year. We were told that they had already been allocated to people with young children, so we had to put up with a little more discomfort than usual.

We had reached Los Angeles, first stop on the journey, before anything else went wrong. The transit desk was a fiasco, with far too much paperwork to be dealt with, and as most of our lads did not have US visas, our tickets had to be produced. They happened to be inconveniently at the bottom of manager A. C. Smith's bag. After struggling to recover them Alan rather testily remarked: 'This is meant to be the most advanced country in the world!'

By the time we touched down in Honolulu we had passed round about four hundred autograph sheets, sat through four films – I watched *The Star Chamber* and *Stroker Ace*, neither of which were Oscar material – and had innumerable meals, snacks and drinks proferred. Amazingly, three of the crew had flown us from Sydney to Auckland on last year's tour, and had a meal out with us a day or so later. It was good to see old friends, especially as they supplied champagne and red New Zealand wine.

On the second leg of the flight I had a chat with Peter Smith, correspondent for the *Daily Mail* and appointed spokesman for the press boys, on the sensitive subject of relations between players and writers. There were problems on the last tour but I pointed out I would give all the journalists my full co-operation unless I heard that any of them were stirring up stories of fictional rifts in the camp. If that happened, they were on their own and could expect no further help. I appreciate what a difficult job the writers have and am well aware that some players take criticism to heart too easily. Any journalist is within his rights if he confines his comments to matters of selection, strategy and form. But if he goes outside those borders he is on dangerous ground.

We lost 30 December, crossing the international dateline during the final leg of the marathon flight. Touchdown was a relief to weary limbs and tired minds.

SATURDAY 31 DECEMBER Light rain was falling on Fiji as we dis-embarked at 4.10 a.m., which was a surprise to us. It was, however, extremely sticky even at that ungodly hour, which was no surprise at all. Acclimatizing on this island will clearly be a force-fed business.

Officials of the local cricket association were on hand to greet us, escorting the squad to our hotel where, despite the time, a three-piece band struck up, a choice of Australian champagne and local fruit juice was offered and we were all festooned with beads.

The hotel turned out to be caribbean in design, the rooms being built in units around the swimming pool, with eating areas on the terrace and outdoor bars – everything, in short, designed to suit the climate. Some of us sampled the breakfast at 6 a.m. before trying to sleep. I managed one sound hour, two more fitfully dozing and then a spell of reading before leaving my room for a wander. Most of the lads were up and about and we simply sat around and chatted superficially in the zombie-like state familiar to all who have experienced jet lag.

A welcoming reception had been set for mid-afternoon, at which A.C. and I had to toast our hosts with the traditional local drink, a non-alcoholic concoction known as Cava, made by dissolving the powdered root of a pepper plant in cold water and then straining it through the bark of the Vau tree. It has a texture like muddy water and has to be swallowed in a single gulp, but tasted surprisingly good. The proceedings included a formal ceremony in which we were presented with a whale tooth, but as the afternoon wore on the clouds dispersed and there were rapid signs of overheating on the brows of many of the lads.

At dinner tonight I was introduced to another of the local delights – the mosquitoes which attack in swarms. More pleasantly, the villagers put on a colourful routine of dancing and singing, which I managed to enjoy before surrendering to drooping eyelids and retiring to bed shortly before nine.

I woke, startled, and lay listening to drumbeats and fireworks. I struggled out of bed to the window in time to see people jumping into the swimming pool. Glancing at my clock I saw that it was precisely midnight, and as sleep left my brain I realized what the fuss was about. I had quite forgotten it was New Year's Eve.

SUNDAY 1 JANUARY There was a strangely unfamiliar feeling when I put on my whites this morning. Not for years, it seems, have I been out of them for so long, and it is a comforting thought that we have a few gentle days on Fiji to oil the rusty parts before embarking on the sterner business.

We had not planned a very demanding practice session for today, which was just as well as the ground set aside for tomorrow's opening game is waterlogged. Norman Gifford found us an alternative base, but it was on such rough grass that serious attempts to bat or bowl were out of the question. We contented ourselves with some fielding games designed to loosen the muscles, and found this was exacting work in the fierce humidity. We were quickly all covered in sweat and my own first impressions are that this island falls somewhere between St Lucia and Colombo for climate – bloody hot. They do, however, have to suffer a remarkable 22 inches of rain in January and if we have much more now, our two games here will be in jeopardy.

As there were no facilities for batting practice, our main batsmen will go into tomorrow's game completely cold, but I did take Graham Dilley, Norman Cowans and Neil Foster aside so that they could turn their arms over a dozen times to ease the risk of straining muscles in the game.

At selection we decided that those who could both bat and bowl – messrs Smith, Marks, Botham and Gatting – would play in both the games here, as would Bob Taylor, David Gower and Nick Cook. The rest of us would play once each. I plan to stand down from Tuesday's game and David will be captain.

There was a relaxed atmosphere this afternoon. Some of the boys had flown to a neighbouring island for lunch, while others dispersed around the pleasant beaches. Being a confirmed anti-sun man I stayed in the hotel. At dinner this evening the main topic of conversation was the voracity of those local mosquitoes. They seem to have taken a particular fancy to the ankles of A.C. and Nick Cook and the backside of Allan Lamb, of which I entirely fail to see the attraction.

MONDAY 2 JANUARY The fact that we won our first game will not rate headlines, but winning it by a margin of 198 runs was at least cause for encouragement. The opposition, a Fijian President's XI, was anything but formidable, so the only conclusions that can safely be drawn are that we shaped up promisingly and did what was required in a very professional manner.

My own day was ruined by an uncharacteristic lapse. Normally, I am careful to the point of pedantic when it comes to protecting myself against the sun, yet this morning, having agreed to an arrangement whereby we would bat first, I went to watch the first hour of the match in a covered stand, with nothing on my head. I had assumed that the roof would provide protection enough, but it did no more than reflect the rays of the sun and by the time I went on to the field later in the day my face was extremely red in more ways than one.

On the field, things went smoothly after the initial anxiety of Ian Botham taking a blow on the hand while having a practice knock on the coir matting wicket used for the match. It proved not serious and, although 'Beefy' himself scored only eight, a powerful century by Mike Gatting was ample compensation. Mike sensibly played himself in before cutting loose in furious style (five sixes and fourteen fours) to reach 142 out of a total of 274 for six in 50 overs. I juse hope he can show similar form when the bowling is more taxing.

With the run-ups on the rough side, and spiked bowling boots not permitted on the matting, I thought it wise to instruct our quicker bowlers to take things very easily. I was especially unhappy about them bowling without proper footwear, but Botham, Dilley and myself all came through unscathed and the target had been confirmed impossible long before Cook came on to mop up the tail with four cheap wickets.

I made my customary early-evening visit to the manager's room, where we decided we should put the accelerator down as soon as we reach New Zealand. Each of the guys will be told what is expected of him and practice will be very much harder. We agreed, however, that today had been a valuable warm-up.

Lamb curry for dinner. We had all eaten better, but I pointed out we could expect a lot worse, come March.

ENGLAND XI v FIJI CA PRESIDENT'S XI
Played at Churchill Park, Laukota, 2 Jan 1984

England XI won by 198 runs

ENGLAND XI 274 for 6 in 50 overs (M. W. Gatting 142, D. W. Randall 33, J. McGoon 3 for 37)

FIJI CA PRESIDENT'S XI 76 in 34 overs (C. A. C. Browne 30, I. T. Botham 3 for 21, N. G. B. Cook 4 for 9)

TUESDAY 3 JANUARY My phone rang at 5.40 a.m. It was A.C., reporting that Norman Cowans had been up all night, sick, and was clearly in no state to play today. We agreed that Dilley should take his place for what was to be a long day. Leaving our hotel in Nandi, which is the island's capital and business centre, we drove through fog to the airport for an early-morning flight up country. We were airborne only twenty minutes, but as the lack of visibility had delayed take-off by twice that time, we were running behind schedule when we boarded a bus for the half-hour road journey to Suva, our base for a day and a night.

Managed a quick breakfast before reporting to the ground, where once again it was pre-ordained that we would bat first. This time, though, things did not go so well. On a pitch less reliable than yesterday's most of the lads had trouble against their slower bowlers. 'Beefy', for whom this might usually have been an opportunity for something spectacular, lost his off stump first ball and after 50 overs we had limped unconvincingly to 146 for nine.

I felt sorry for David, having to defend such a total. But, although the locals put up a much better fight than in the first game, I never thought we were in serious danger as, avoiding yesterday's folly, I sheltered in a rare patch of shade under some trees. An eighth-wicket stand of 51 brought them within striking distance of what would have been cause for massive local celebrations, but when Dilley and Foster came back into the attack, the last three wickets fell on the same score and we had won by 18 runs. It was an escape from the first minor crisis of the tour, but if all are overcome so painlessly we will go home happy.

As this was our last night in Fiji, a reception was laid on at which the staff of our hotel launched into a dancing session and managed to persuade us all to join in. It was probably amusing viewing, but we made up in enthusiasm what we patently lacked in expertise.

ENGLAND XI v FIJI CA PRESIDENT'S XI
Played at Albert Park, Suva, 3 Jan 1984

England XI won by 18 runs

ENGLAND XI 146 for 9 in 50 overs (A. J. Lamb 35, C. L. Smith 30)

FIJI CA PRESIDENT'S XI 128 in 48.2 overs (N. G. B. Cook 4 for 20)

WEDNESDAY 4 JANUARY Four days and nights have not cured my jetlag. I am still waking like clockwork at three in the morning and the thick novel I brought out with me – *Worldly Goods* by Michael Korda – is finished already. I failed to complete a single book in Australia last winter but I have found reading an enjoyable way of resting on this tour, even if I do crave a better sleeping pattern.

My fried face, I notice, has lost its glow but there are distinct signs that I will be peeling soon. I really mustn't get caught like that again.

As this morning was free, prior to our flight back to Nandi and subsequent trip on to Auckland, A.C. and I took the chance to have a talk with Ian. He is seldom out of the news, and in the days leading up to the tour he apparently ignored TCCB pleas to pull out of Scunthorpe United's two Christmas league matches. He is much taken by his soccer career and, although I could not officially con-done his actions, it seemed to be entirely a matter for the Board and I was just thankful that he had come through unscathed and now looked in good physical shape. We told him that we were looking for a positive contribution and stressed how important it was that he set a good example at practice over the next fortnight as the side begins to knit together. He gave us no flannel; on the contrary, he was very receptive, saying that he felt extremely fit and that he was confident his bowling would be back to its old self, outswinger fully restored.

When Ian had left us, I filled in A.C. on some of the things we could expect to confront us in New Zealand, a place he has not visited for twenty years since playing two Tests there on the 1962–63 tour. I told him that the airport agricultural checks were stringent, that the umpiring had recently been of modest standard and that the cricket officials were likely to be stubborn in their views about playing conditions. They are nice folk, but inclined to be obstinate.

Once we had returned to Nandi, by way of a sixteen-seater light aircraft which necessitated the baggage following on by the next plane, I called a team meeting and explained similar details to the players, few of whom have ever been to New Zealand. I also told them that I felt we should have a social committee. Last year in Australia, this was largely self-elected and concentrated on Christmas activities. This year, although we had missed Christmas, I thought we should aim to have three functions – one at the end of our stay in New Zealand, a second in Faisalabad where time is bound to drag, and a final party just prior to leaving Pakistan. I had already given the make-up of the committee some thought and proposed Vic Marks, Graeme Fowler and Neil Foster. Two of them have made one tour each, Foster is a new boy and none of the three feature among the most gregarious or extrovert in the squad. It was for these reasons that they were selected and, although each in turn looked taken aback, none of them were unwilling.

Our flight to Auckland took three hours. Customs was cleared surprisingly swiftly and it was then all hands to the pump again, lifting our fifty-four pieces of luggage off the carousel and on to the bus for the twenty-minute drive to the Sheraton Hotel in the city centre. First impressions are good – I am not used to five-star hotels in New Zealand, but this one looks exceptional. I still found cause to change my room as I had been given a single bed, which I always find cramping. They immediately relocated me in a room with an enormous seven-foot-square bed.

THURSDAY 5 JANUARY A sports presenter from 2KY, one of Sydney's many commercial radio stations, phoned early this morning asking for my reaction to the news that both Dennis Lillee and Greg Chappell have announced their retirement from international cricket. Forced to quantify my feelings without time for reflection,

I praised them both as cricketers of the very highest calibre. What I did not say is that neither of their personalities have been untarnished – Lillee has been the central figure in some unacceptable incidents on the field and some notorious episodes off it (remember the bet against his own side at Leeds in 1981?), while Chappell's elegant and dignified appearance belied, in my view, a sometimes unpleasantly caustic side.

I have nothing but admiration for their ability, however, and especially for Dennis's fortitude in the face of back injuries which would have put paid to most careers. He is the finest fast bowler I have ever seen and he now stands deservedly well clear at the top of the table of Test wicket-takers with 355. When this tour began I would have said I had no chance of overhauling him, as I expected him to go on playing a while longer, still taking wickets with that economical style which relies more on his ability to make the ball swing and seam than on his old ally of sheer pace. I knew, and still know, that I could never operate like that – once my speed goes, my effect goes with it – but, here I am, with 305 wickets banked, 50 behind Dennis, and no immediate plans to quit. Perhaps there is a chance of the record, after all.

The one-hour time change meant that I slept until four instead of three this morning but I was still able to get some way into my second book of the tour, Jeffrey Archer's *Kane and Abel*, before breakfast. We had a satisfactory session in the nets, most of the batters having two innings each and the bowlers working for almost two hours, all of us finding the temperature and humidity far more comfortable for cricket than it had been in Fiji.

Radio and television interviewers were waiting for me after nets. It is already quite noticeable that the country's interest in cricket is much higher than when we last visited for a Test series, six years ago.

After soaking in a lunchtime bath, listening to Wagner's 'The Golden Ring', I told the seam bowlers to rest while half a dozen of the other lads returned for further net practice. They have done enough for the first day of serious exercise.

My fears about the stubbornness of officials here seem well-founded. We met some of them at a reception tonight, and they made it plain they would not be interested in playing a minimum 96 overs a day – the regulation we operated with some success in England last summer. It's a pity, but not a great surprise.

FRIDAY 6 JANUARY Woke to the sound of rain battering against the windows of my bedroom, which was exactly what we did not want on Day Two of the tour proper. 'Giff', doing the reconnaissance job once carried out so capably and enthusiastically by the late Kenny Barrington, came back from an early trip to the ground with news that facilities were available for indoor practice, so we kept to the originally planned timings and, in the circumstances, put in two hours of useful work.

My lunchtime soak was today accompanied by Mozart's 23rd piano concerto, soothing background while I contemplated selection for the first three-day game which begins tomorrow. When I met with the other selectors, we decided that the four men to be left out should be Smith, Randall, Cowans and Marks. We considered that Dilley needed a full match off his long run as he was suffering from no-ball problems at practice yesterday. This means 'Flash' Cowans is still waiting to start his competitive tour, but we are not in an ideal world and certainly do not have an ideal itinerary.

Early this evening, the press laid on an informal drinks party for us. A.C. and I arrived a short while before the other players so that we could chat generally about arrangements for press conferences for the tour. It also gave me the opportunity to stress my view that they were entitled to write that I could not captain a rowing boat but not that I was having some fictional row with another member of the party. I am afraid the worry about this possibility still preys on my mind.

Had a drink later on at a bar called Wyndhams, which is apparently where Auckland's action is to be found. The years, however, have caught up with me. Bars where the music is loud and the drinks extortionate no longer stimulate me and I retreated early, went back for a bite of dinner in my room and could not even stay awake for a Clint Eastwood film on the hotel video.

SATURDAY 7 JANUARY It was a patchy, puzzling way for us to start the serious cricket of the tour but I cannot imagine that many of the 8000-plus crowd left Eden Park tonight disappointed with the entertainment value. Briefly, we were bowled out for 220 despite a breathtaking innings of 84 from Gower, then hit back well to take five Auckland wickets for 109 by the close.

The day emphasized we have much work still to do, and perhaps some of it should concentrate on attitude. Certain of our batsmen got themselves out playing in a needlessly arrogant manner. I realize that the bowling of Sean Tracy, Gary Troup and Martin Snedden did not look great, but some of our blokes treated them with contempt and paid the price – Snedden took six wickets, which will probably help him into the side for the First Test.

We had won the toss and, on an evenly-grassed pitch, I was happy to bat first, yet our entire innings resembled a 50-overs slog. Gower is exempt from criticism, and Mike Gatting again played well for 56, but most were caught in front of the wicket playing forcing shots rather than being genuinely got out.

'Beefy' looked lbw to the third ball he received. Given the benefit of the doubt – if there was any doubt – he was then promptly hit on the toe. Not only was this one given out, but the swelling kept him off the field later in the day. Early on during most tours, I do feel Ian tends to play across the line, and needs to get into the rhythm of hitting straight.

I took things very easily when we bowled. I intend to play in all three of the first-class games prior to the Wellington Test and it is pointless trying to rush in at full speed and getting injured at this stage.

The team-room tonight was riotously funny. Ian was christened 'run-machine' after his second successive nought, and there was a session of near-the-knuckle mickey-taking, accepted in good part by all concerned. Chat then inevitably got around to Pakistan, prompted by a bout of sickness suffered by Bob Taylor last night. 'Giff' was in great form with his stories of previous trips to that part of the world. This was an hour and a half of amusement, everyone together and in good spirits. It was what touring should be all about.

Dined with 'Giff', who said he thought Gower was now on a par with anyone in the world, so early does he pick up the ball. Had a drink in the bar and went to bed quite early.

SUNDAY 8 JANUARY John Bracewell survived a blatant bat-pad catch while on two today. He went on to score a hundred – with a six hooked off my bowling – and the eyes of many of our younger players were thus opened to what may well be one of our major problems this series. New Zealand umpires are simply not of comparable standard to ours at home – not surprising bearing in mind their comparative lack of opportunity at first-class level. The Bracewell incident was a very easy decision to give and I'm afraid the man responsible for what, to my mind, was plainly a mistake was Fred Goodall, their best umpire. It is important that our lads do not allow these things to upset them and appreciate that it is certainly not the umpires' impartiality which is at question – bad decisions will go both ways, as yesterday's leg-before reprieve for Botham stressed.

It was irritating, nonetheless. We had looked to be well on top after taking another early wicket this morning but Bracewell and Martin Snedden shared such an effective stand that Auckland were able to declare 63 ahead. The compensation is that our bowlers all had a good workout – all, that is, except 'Beefy', still confined to the dressing-room by his toe injury. We ended the day on 100 for four, only narrowly ahead and in a mess with regard to this game, though I am certainly not yet panicking in terms of our Test preparation.

Tonight's talk got around to racing, one of my favourite subjects, and in particular the Cheltenham Gold Cup, staged in mid-March. 'Giff' and I disagreed with Ian and the MCC president Alex Dibbs who, on visiting the team-room, declared his fancy for Fred Winter's Fifty Dollars More. Neither Norman nor I consider the horse is good enough and we laid bets for both his supporters, at generous odds. When the race is run, we will be sampling the delights of Faisalabad. No doubt a phone call home will be in order, to sort out the financial details!

Sunday evening in Auckland is anything but lively and certain of the players and journalists resorted to a game of charades in the lobby bar.

MONDAY 9 JANUARY The first unwanted ripple to disturb the morale of the tour seems to centre on me. Alan Smith summoned me at breakfast time to tell me that an English businessman has complained about the behaviour of the team in the hotel. The man has gone further, telexing his remarks to the *Daily Express* in London and naming Ian Botham, Allan Lamb and myself in connection with alleged 'drunken and surly behaviour' until 1 a.m. on Saturday night. He also claims that Ian's absence from the field must be due to a hangover.

I could only tell Alan the truth, which is that the incidents referred to never occurred. Yes, all three of us were in the hotel bar that evening. But Allan left at 9.50 p.m., I went to bed at 10.15 p.m. and Ian left just after 11.00 p.m., when the bar *shut*. It was physically impossible for us to have been drinking there past that hour as no more drinks were served.

At the ground this morning Pat Gibson, the *Daily Express* writer on the tour, showed me a copy of the telex, which as far as I am concerned is Cinderella stuff without the slightest substance. I was able to meet the businessman, who goes by the name of Brooks, to say that I strongly denied and objected to his accusations. But I fear the damage has been done; this evening I heard that the story had been printed in the *Express* although, on Pat Gibson's protestations, it had been considerably muted.

The press party with us were understandably in a flap about it all, under pressure from their respective offices to write follow-ups, and poor A.C. got himself rather worked up. I was extremely angry this morning but I can now at least see the farcical side of it, having watched journalists going up and down in the hotel lift, knocking on Mr Brooks's door and vainly trying to get a comment from him. He now says the press are harassing him. Does it not occur to him he has harassed us? Fortunately for my own peace of mind with regard to tomorrow's papers, at least three of the journalists had been in the bar throughout our stay that evening and confirm that they saw nothing untoward at all.

Such things we can well do without, but at least the day was not all bad. Thanks to tenacious batting from 'Gatt' and Bob Taylor, both of whom made half-centuries, we comfortably saved the game. We were eventually bowled out after tea, 258 ahead, and although I was heartily booed when I went out to bat for declining to declare, there had never been any realistic chance of us winning in the time remaining so the option was barely worth considering.

It was a relief not to start with a defeat, especially one which

---

ENGLAND XI v AUCKLAND

Played at Eden Park, Auckland, 7, 8, 9 Jan 1984

Drawn

ENGLAND XI 220 (D. I. Gower 84, M. W. Gatting 56, M. C. Snedden 6 for 70) and 321 (R. W. Taylor 86, M. W. Gatting 64, I. T. Botham 44)

AUCKLAND 283 for 8 dec (J. G. Bracewell 104 not out, J. F. Reid 43) and 58 for 1 (P. N. Webb 41 not out)

would have been rather unjust. Tomorrow we fly to Palmerston North, and I hope we shall be leaving Mr Brooks behind.

TUESDAY 10 JANUARY No developments on the 'drunkards' story. Hopefully it will now die a deserved death.

Palmerston North, like most other places near the foot of North Island, was being battered by a strong wind when we arrived, but the sun was shining, facilities at the ground were good and we were able to conduct a satisfactory practice session during the afternoon.

The Fitzherbert Hotel, our home for the next three nights, is perfectly comfortable, my one reservation being the lack of a bath in the rooms. Fast bowlers traditionally like to soak away the aches of the day and I am no exception. A shower, I find, is no real substitute.

I discovered tonight that the restaurant here is not among the best we have come across. We were asked to wait a long time for a table – and suffered the obvious amusing innuendoes about the sight of messrs Botham, Lamb and Willis having a drink in the bar – and then sat down to an unspectacular meal. Still, as I keep reminding myself, it was the sort of food we would be singing about in two months' time.

Our match with Central Districts begins tomorrow. Gower and Gatting, who have proved their form with the bat, stand down along with Foster, who has already got through plenty of work. 'Foxy' Fowler is given another chance to make a decent score, albeit out of position at three, and 'Flash' Cowans plays his first game of the tour.

WEDNESDAY 11 JANUARY I was busying myself about my usual morning routine of collecting together the laundry when my wife phoned from Birmingham. It sounds as if she is being well looked after by various of our friends, and there are no complications with the forthcoming nipper as yet. It is good to get such news, as we could hardly be further apart geographically.

Won the toss again and batted on a good-looking pitch. 'Kippy' Smith was out early but Chris Tavaré spent a long time at the crease and 'Foxy' played his shots, which I think is what he has decided he must do. He tends to miss the ball a good deal outside off stump, in the style of many a left-hander, but he looks a good player when attacking. He has played long enough now to work out the style which suits him best and it is not up to me to tell him how he should bat.

Ian recovered some semblance of form with a spectacular half-hour of hitting and Derek Randall played well enough for a while. I declared when he was out and we had seventy minutes in the field, during which I felt we bowled far more impressively than in Auckland. I bowled six overs, seeking rhythm and concentrating on line and length and generally feeling much fitter and more capable than in previous games.

The spirit of this squad is pleasing. They want to work, they want to be fit – and how good it is to see 'Beefy' shaking off the accusations which have previously hung around him in this regard and looking so trim. He was one of four who ran the mile back from ground to hotel tonight, the others being Fowler, Smith and Lamb.

Had an after-dinner drink in the bar to ensure all was quiet. It sounds absurd, having to adopt such a matronly approach, but Mr Brooks might just have clones in other parts of New Zealand and we want to avoid any more such stories.

THURSDAY 12 JANUARY One look outside my window this morning confirmed that it had been raining virtually all night. A.C. and 'Giff' went off early to inspect the ground and returned with news that the practice facilities were awash. We delayed our departure until 10.00 a.m. and I had time to read the local morning paper, which praised us for the approach and style of our batting yesterday.

Surprisingly, the square was perfectly playable and we resumed on time, Vic Marks taking five wickets as Central Districts were dismissed quite cheaply. (One of his wickets was courtesy of a spectacular acrobatic catch by 'Arkle' at deep midwicket off a low sweep shot by Ian Smith – one of the best catches any of us have seen him make.) 'Skid' has yet to prove he can be a consistent wicket-taker at Test level but he is clearly not out here as a spare part. We lost three second-innings wickets before reaching 50, Chris Smith failing for the second time in the game, but Fowler and Randall were in control by the end of another pretty pleasing day.

As a change from what had become a predictable routine of drinking in the team-room and eating in the hotel, I went to a barbecue tonight. It was run by some of the hotel staff, just a couple of blocks up the road, and despite the usual strong wind buffetting us around, it was an enjoyable break.

FRIDAY 13 JANUARY The thermal vest and long johns came out today as we were obliged to brave some of the worst conditions I can remember for cricket. Apart from one occasion in Tasmania, when play was actually halted by a gale, this was the strongest and most unmanageable wind in which I have played. It blew straight down the ground and brought hats, beer cans and paper whisking across the pitch at regular intervals. In the circumstances, none of us were sorry when stumps were drawn on a deadlocked game at 5.30 p.m. and we could hurry back to the relative calm and warmth of the dressing-room.

'Giff' had needed to chivvy us into our fielding practice this morning and was right to do so. It has been bearing fruit in terms of catches taken, although it is interesting that there has not yet been a single slip catch from our bowling on the tour.

We batted until lunch, piling up an unassailable lead of almost 400. After Fowler had completed a very good hundred, Botham and Randall set about the bowling in a manner reminiscent of their marvellous stand in the Trent Bridge Test last summer. Ian scored 80 in about forty-five minutes, enjoying himself hugely, and if the bowling they faced towards the end of the demolition was far from hostile, it was at least a worthwhile exercise in crease-occupation and confidence-building.

Bowling with the wind at my back after lunch, I was satisfied with myself, except for the constant concern of a deep and rough foot-hold just where my front boot liked to pound down in the delivery stride. This crater caused further problems later: 'Picca' Dilley was regularly inconvenienced as he landed on the downward slope and slipped, and Ian twisted his knee in it and had to leave the field.

'Skid' gamely bowled into the hurricane for most of the afternoon

---

ENGLAND XI v CENTRAL DISTRICTS

Played at Palmerston North, 11, 12, 13 Jan 1984

Drawn

ENGLAND XI 294 for 6 dec (C. J. Tavaré 89, G. Fowler 83, A. J. Lamb 51) and 300 for 6 dec (G. Fowler 104, I. T. Botham 80, D. W. Randall 66)

CENTRAL DISTRICTS 168 (M. D. Crowe 41, V. J. Marks 5 for 66) and 162 for 2 (R. T. Hart 67, P. S. Briasco 65 not out)

---

but we never looked like winning. What had seemed a long and unfriendly day was lengthened further by a travel change which meant we had to fly to Hamilton via Wellington, so it was 11 p.m. by the time we arrived at our motel-style base.

SATURDAY 14 JANUARY Hotels like this are not geared up to cater for parties like ours. There is no bar, and breakfast has to be ordered the previous night and brought to the rooms. Mine arrived just before 7.30 a.m. and was quickly discarded – I have never been a fan of 'Skippy' corn flakes, and the bacon and eggs wore an inedibly leathery look. I drank the orange juice and went back to bed for an hour.

Before leaving for the ground, and another playing day, I did a radio interview with a girl from the local station. She complained that Hamilton was a very quiet place with little to do after ten at night but, with the First Test less than a week away now, I can't help feeling that may not be a bad thing for our blokes.

At the ground I met up with my Test opposite number and long-time buddy Geoff Howarth for the first time since our arrival. We went out to toss together, Geoff being captain of Northern Districts, and for the third time in succession I called right and chose to bat. I can only hope the run continues.

Chris Smith quickly added to our healthy selection complications, leaving his Palmerston disappointments well behind with an impressive century. Once he got his timing right he never looked likely to get out, and I am struck by his ability to retain concentration for long periods. Like Boycott, he relishes long innings and if he can keep this form he will be a valuable lynchpin. As 'Arkle' Randall also got a decent score, all our batsmen have runs in the bank prior to the First Test, an unusual state of affairs on any tour.

While watching the lads batting I consulted various senior players to seek their views on the competition for Test places. It was interesting to listen to the conflicting views from around the dressing-room on the respective merits of, for instance, spinners Marks and Cook and pace bowlers Dilley and Cowans. Selection will clearly not be easy.

We bowled for fifty minutes tonight and ran into a local difficulty: it is practically impossible to gain an lbw verdict here if the batsman is hit on the front pad. We must accept it and try not to get agitated, but it is hard when we are so used to a different, and I think more logical, form of umpiring which penalises batsmen who shuffle their front pad just outside the crease and use the bat as a second line of defence.

A team meeting this evening was illuminating. After I had said it was time to toughen ourselves up in the field and become more competitive in support of the bowlers, appealing convincingly when a man looked out, Chris Tavaré raised some good points about field settings. There is a general feeling that our fields are often too attacking, conceding needless runs, and I would go along with this view.

Dined with A.C., 'Giff' and David Gower across the road from the hotel, at reputedly Hamilton's best restaurant. It was good, albeit with slightly slow service, but after sharing a bottle of Australian claret I got to thinking that I must watch my intake of food and drink from now on. I am showing no signs of losing weight and it is certainly not the time to put any on. It is far too easy, when on tour, to eat three substantial meals a day without doing the exercise to earn them.

SUNDAY 15 JANUARY Every Sunday morning on tour you can guarantee there will be a dressing-room inquest on the soccer scores from England. Today, the unexpected demise of Liverpool, at home to Wolves, caused consternation for some; and 'Arkle' was the subject of ribbing for his usual habit of claiming to support whichever of the Nottingham teams has won. I was pleased to hear that my team, Manchester City, had won three–one, but can't help fearing they will miss out on promotion.

On the field, all went according to plan. Ian had a long bowl, did not get bored and resort to his short run, and looked pretty useful. The day's star, however, was Neil Foster, who picked up career-best figures of six for 30. His control is so good, but I wish he would not try to drop in the odd short ball. He is not quick enough for it to be effective and, more often than not, it is dispatched for four. I can't carp about him too much today, though.

I decided against enforcing the follow-on because I wanted our openers to have another knock. 'Tav', however, was out early again before Smith and Randall took up where they had left off in the first innings, Chris scoring 50 and Derek a fine century.

We were 370 runs on at stumps and as I lay in the bath listening to Bob Dylan on my tape machine I could reflect on a happy position. There was also a hilarious evening to come – the first meeting called by our new social committee. Fines were imposed on almost everybody, in order to raise funds for our later parties, and this evening's business brought in 86 New Zealand dollars. Those who were fined for their misdemeanours included the entire management, for booking the lads into a hotel with no bar; Norman Gifford, for an excessively sunburned face; Bernard Thomas, for driving his borrowed car the wrong way round a central reservation in Auckland; and Chris Tavaré, for his custom of wearing pyjamas. Messrs Marks, Foster and Fowler have entered into the spirit of their position and done well. With so few gaffes being missed, however, I think they are now unpopular room-mates!

MONDAY 16 JANUARY A drawn game seemed predictable, despite my overnight declaration, but although we did win in the last half hour, I was concerned by a lethargy which crept into our play this afternoon. Okay, the pitch was flat and slow and batsmen had little trouble surviving – which was their primary aim all day – but Nick Cook was getting some turn, yet still bowled an average of two bad balls an over. I was suffering no-ball problems, something I have learned to live with over the years, and Ian was probably the pick of our bowlers.

All that can be said is that we came through our first full day in the field without injury, and we will be fitter and better prepared now for what lies ahead. I told the press tonight that we were in the almost unique situation, in my experience, of having every member of a tour party in contention for a Test place. I was not able to give them any more clues.

ENGLAND XI v NORTHERN DISTRICTS
Played at Hamilton, 14, 15, 16 Jan 1984

England XI won by 77 runs

ENGLAND XI 287 for 3 dec (C. L. Smith 138 not out, D. I. Gower 69) and 194 for 2 dec (D. W. Randall 101 not out, C. L. Smith 50)

NORTHERN DISTRICTS 111 (N. A. Foster 6 for 30) and 293 (C. M. Presland 58, A. D. G. Roberts 58, G. P. Howarth 55, I. T. Botham 4 for 72, N. G. B. Cook 4 for 91)

3

A TALE OF
LOST OPPORTUNITIES

TUESDAY 17 JANUARY There is little enough opportunity for practice on this tour already. Now, it seems, the weather has joined the conspiracy against us. Even before we boarded our flight this morning, we were told that Wellington had suffered so much rain that an afternoon net session was out of the question. We witnessed the truth of that when we stepped off the plane. It was still raining, it was 9 degrees centigrade and felt much colder. To sum up, the weather was wretched and our spirits sank.

It had started out as an enjoyable day. 'Beefy' Botham, Norman Gifford and myself, the three racing afficionados in the party, left the hotel after an early breakfast to visit the Middle Park stud, about eight miles out of Hamilton. The main object of our curiosity was the stallion Balmarino. He finished second to Alleged in the 1977 Prix de l'Arc de Triomphe, probably the world's most prestigious flat race, yet he was standing at a comparatively meagre 15,000 New Zealand dollars. There is clearly some good horse business to be done in New Zealand.

We were a little like rudderless ships this afternoon, three days away from a Test and deprived of precious practice, but I called the lads together for a pep-talk. I told them that after tonight I wanted to see appreciably less drinking and socializing and more early nights. I am seldom up late to go around checking the bars, nor would I consider it the right thing to do, but I thought it worth stressing that, after a relatively leisurely warm-up period, Test cricket could come as a shock to certain systems.

A.C. returned from the Test ground with the disturbing news that the match wicket was awash. Incomprehensibly, it was not covered during the storms they had here on Monday night and, in Alan's opinion, it had little chance of drying out by Friday. I felt angry about this apparent negligence – something which, as A.C. was quick to point out, simply would not happen before a Test in England – but with the game still three days away it is best to say nothing.

I made it clear that the lads could enjoy themselves tonight and it was good to see that spirits were high in the team-room. 'Arkle' was in one of his uninhibited, comic moods as we recalled the pig which was set loose on the Brisbane ground last winter, 'Botham' painted on one side and 'Eddie' (Hemmings) on the other. I was able to take the tale a stage further as I subsequently met the guys responsible – a pair of vets, who put the pig in a freezer box with an apple in his mouth. Apparently the gateman, having insisted that the box be opened, prodded the animal dubiously and said it didn't look very well cooked!

WEDNESDAY 18 JANUARY It would seem that Geoff Howarth is just as unhappy as us over the state of the Test ground. I met up with my opposite number and old friend at tonight's British High Commission reception and he made it clear that leaving pitches uncovered was certainly not his idea of being clever. It is apparently not the first time it has happened here, nor the first time that G. P. Howarth has voiced his disapproval of uncovered wickets.

Alan Smith's enquiries this morning had confirmed his suspicions that the entire area was open to the worst of the weather and, at our lunchtime briefing for the British press, A.C. stated his disappointment and concern. No doubt it has given the writers something to get their teeth into on an otherwise quiet day.

The nets were, unsurprisingly, still far too wet for use today and we had to improvize; Ian led some of the lads in a session of running around the ground, while the rest of the squad practised indoors. I conducted my own practice, bowling off a decent run on the side of the square, A.C. wearing the gloves at the other end. It may have helped smooth out my run-up, but I could not be sure. Bowling without a batsman can put you in a fool's paradise and even induce bad habits, but with two days left before the Test begins and no chance of authentic practice it was at least better than nothing.

After three weeks away, I am very happy with the general morale of the side and especially with the way the three new guys have fitted in. I never had serious doubts about messrs Smith, Foster and Cook but it is still a relief to see them adapting to this rather foreign existence. Chris, who comes from a wealthy South African family background, is not as extrovert as his fellow countryman Allan Lamb but he is nonetheless a positive and very dedicated team-man. 'Kippy' is his usual nickname but he has been called

'Dredger' and 'Oil Rig' on occasions when, burdened with the helmet at short-leg, he has looked particularly immobile. Neil, nicknamed 'Hermann' because he has been rebuilt like Mr Munster and has the scars to prove it, is lively and opinionated. His country accent brings him no end of mickey-taking but he accepts it all in good part. Most impressive of all is his appetite for learning about the game. Nick, a livewire character, is an ideal tourist. He has palled up with Mike Gatting and philosophically answers to the name 'Beast'. I must find out why. He is not bowling as well as he can but at least he is aware of it.

We are not yet committed to an eleven for the Test but it does seem likely that all three of the new boys will play.

THURSDAY 19 JANUARY I can hardly recall a more unsatisfactory build-up to a Test series. The three days we had allotted for practice have been aborted because of the ground conditions and today, once again, we were restricted to a few stretches, some half-cock efforts indoors and – for myself – a further forty-five minutes bowling on the outfield, none of which will guarantee us starting this series in peak condition. The weather in Wellington is fickle: the wind here is strong almost all the time; when it does drop, it rains. Those who complain so much about the English climate would do so no more after a few weeks here. But, having admitted all the problems, I still cannot help feeling we have been hard done by.

The selectors met at lunchtime. There was virtually no discussion over seven of the places but the rest caused considerable debate. Of the opening batsmen, Tavaré has been in poor form but is proven at the highest level, Smith is a dour sticker with a recent century and Fowler scored 83 and 104 against Central Districts. We could only choose two of them and, with the damp pitch in mind, opted for durability ahead of flair and left out Fowler. Dilley was the unlucky fast bowler and Cook got the nod over Marks for the spin place.

I have seldom reached the first Test of a tour with every member of the party in good enough form to demand consideration. It is a healthy way to be so long as the blokes who are left out respond in the right way. When we announced the twelve to the lads this afternoon I made a point of saying that the three omitted were all very unlucky. I will speak individually to them later.

The guys were all in positive mood at our eve-of-Test gathering tonight, which made for heartening listening. Although we have recently seen a good deal of the New Zealanders, we chatted through the strengths and weaknesses of them all, concluding that, of their batsmen, Wright, Edgar, Coney and Hadlee had caused us the most trouble in previous encounters. I said we should all be careful not to underestimate their back-up bowlers just because they appear to be so inferior to Hadlee. Complacency is so often the biggest enemy of a batsman, just as confidence is his greatest friend.

Went to bed directly after dinner and, as usual during a match, asked the operator to field any calls until 7.30 a.m.

FRIDAY 20 JANUARY Today I became England's leading wicket-taker in Test history. For all my misgivings about the value of statistics, all my protestations that I am not a records man, I found that I was very conscious of counting down to the record as I took the three wickets necessary and, perhaps more surprising, I also found that I was very moved by the whole occasion. For a change, I really did savour the moment as it happened, relishing the genuinely enthusiastic congratulations of the other lads, appreciating the gesture of Richard Hadlee in coming to meet me and shake my hand as we left the field, and enjoying the taste and the meaning of the champagne which Alan Smith had poured in readiness. In some ways I would consider it the highlight of my career. A lot of work and a good deal of pain has gone into the taking of 308 wickets and it was especially good to share the moment with Ian Botham and Bob Taylor, two friends who have been very much part of the scenery while I have taken the majority of them.

Fred Trueman held the record for twenty years but I doubt if whatever mark I set will stand for anything like another twenty. I. T. Botham is hot on the trail and no one will be more pleased than me if, having passed my total, he goes on to break Dennis Lillee's world record. Ian's effort, motivation and, as usual, company have been marvellous on this trip and, although this will go down as my day, he and Neil Foster were the heroes who put in the hard slog to get us off to such a pleasing start to the series. At the end of the day, New Zealand were 212 for nine on a pitch which turned out to be slow and far from menacing, the ball not seaming as much as we thought it might.

My pre-match routine had been improved by an unusually good night's sleep – seven and a half hours, pretty near my personal best for the night before a Test! Julie phoned at 7.45 a.m. and I was pleased to hear her report that all was well, apart from the garden fence having blown down! After breakfast I put the 'Do Not Disturb' sign on my door and spent half an hour listening, for the first time, to a new hypnosis tape sent by Arthur Jackson from Sydney. It did not get rid of my nerves, which are an important part of any sportsman's make-up, but it did send me off in a more positive, clear-thinking mood.

As usual, the selectors met on the pitch an hour before the start. Instead of being the traditional sanctuary in which only match officials and the odd television camerman is permitted, the area was a chaotic free-for-all and our elbows were constantly being nudged by autograph hunters while we were trying to pick the side.

We left out Cowans and decided we should bat first, given the option. The wicket was still moist, albeit less so than we had feared, and inevitably looked underprepared for a five-day Test.

Geoff Howarth joined me and tossed a ten-cent coin. I called heads, it came down tails and, despite having left out their one spinner, Evan Gray, he too had decided that batting first was the thing to do.

On reflection, I think our faster bowlers – myself included – fell into the trap of 'putting' the ball on the spot and expecting it to move, rather than seeking speed and life. Although we did not achieve much lateral movement we did succeed in tying down the early Kiwi batsmen and, eventually, began working through them.

'Beefy' got both the openers with short balls, Wright caught at mid-on off a mis-hit and Edgar caught behind while trying to hook. They fell at 34 and 39 and, although it had taken us more than ninety minutes to achieve the break-through, I felt we had bowled and fielded in a very professional manner.

Just after lunch we picked up an especially pleasing third wicket. We always fancy getting Howarth caught in the gully region as he plays rather loosely through that area. Sure enough, he obliged by slicing a drive to Gower. It was 56 for three and all three wickets to Botham.

When I chipped in by bowling Martin Crowe we were very much in command, but Jeff Crowe and Jerry Coney held us up, Coney playing solidly while Crowe survived more than his share of air shots outside off stump. Nick Cook split them, having a disbelieving Coney adjudged caught bat-pad, and 'Fozzy' Foster then bowled quite superbly at Hadlee for one in only his second Test. It was a long spell of very mature bowling which included the wicket of Crowe but not of Hadlee. When Foster rested after drinks in the last session, however, Hadlee was immediately out to Ian, for which Foster must take most of the credit.

I have never seen a player quite like Hadlee. He looks terrified of anything above medium pace and was often extremely uncomfortable against 'Fozzy', particularly against the short pitched ball. Yet he makes major scores by striking the ball so cleanly and remains a very great danger.

By contrast with messrs Botham and Foster, Cook was unimpressive today. He bowled a long and resolute spell but was hit both sides of the wicket, indicating that his line was not what it should have been. New Zealand were never in a strong enough position to chance their arm against the spinner, which was as well for us.

Taking the new ball towards the end of the day, I picked up the eighth and ninth wickets myself – Martin Snedden caught behind and Lance Cairns superbly held at third slip by Gatting, who had put him down in my first over back. This last wicket was the record-breaker, and a great feeling it was too. The milestone was announced on the loudspeaker and I confess to feeling quite touched by the reception. Back in the dressing-room, Bob Taylor led the lads in a chorus of 'For he's a jolly good fellow'. Champagne glasses were raised. The Kiwis came in to shake my hand. A marvellous day. I went back to sing Dylan in the bath, reflecting on the irony that my greatest achievement had come on a day when I felt terribly rusty through lack of practice. Such is cricket.

SATURDAY 21 JANUARY We ended the second day on 293 for five, a lead of 74 and a powerful if not yet decisive advantage. I could not be more pleased, especially as the central character today was Botham, dominating proceedings as we all know he can. He took five wickets in the New Zealand innings and he has followed that with an unbeaten hundred. Just to prove beyond doubt that this is vintage Botham, he even had the odd slice of luck – dropped at slip by Cairns before he had scored; then dropped again at 19 and 75.

I had slept badly. A phone call somehow slipped through the switchboard net to wake me at 12.30 a.m. and, although I drifted back to sleep, I was fully awake again soon after five. It quite often happens early in a season or early in a tour, when the body is rebelling against new demands being put on it. At least I was not alone. Neil Foster ambled into breakfast with very similar complaints.

Bernard Thomas massaged my stiff back before play began but we were not long delayed, 'Beefy' rapidly having Smith lbw after I had induced Chatfield to give a catch off a no ball – one of a bowler's greatest frustrations. The total of 219 was not formidable but neither could it be considered a disaster. I don't expect this pitch to get much better and it is entirely possible that the bounce could be uneven on the last day or so.

Midway through the afternoon session, indeed, that New Zealand score had begun to assume very respectable proportions. We had lost our first five wickets for 115 and were making very heavy weather of the job after an encouragingly steady first-wicket stand of 41. Cairns bowled well, swinging the ball late and taking all the early wickets, but there were some needless dismissals too. I sat and suffered through every ball, as did almost everyone else in the squad. There was not much conversation, just the usual, noticeable tension while things went wrong, lifting slowly into a more relaxed atmosphere as messrs Botham and Randall came – not for the first time – to our rescue.

Cairns wheeled on without his early breaks, Chatfield was steady, Hadlee we played well. Gradually, from the brink of crisis, we achieved respect and then strength. By the close, Ian and Derek had put on 178.

At five o'clock, Vic Marks, as acting twelfth man, had taken out the drinks. Ian was in the eighties and 'Skid' asked if I wanted to pass on any messages. 'Yes,' I replied. 'Tell him to concentrate, play straight and think how many players have scored thirteen Test hundreds.' A few minutes later I had my reply. 'He says you know he can't concentrate, he's never played straight in his life and he couldn't give a damn how many blokes have got thirteen hundreds.' It was a typically irrepressible Botham answer, but maybe some of the message got through. As 'Skid' remarked thoughtfully at the end of the day, he did play straighter and he did get his hundred.

I played Van Morrison in the bath and enjoyed it enormously. Every player came to the team-room for a hilarious twenty minutes of in-jokes. Touring can seem a good life while things go well on the field.

SUNDAY 22 JANUARY Our day again, beyond question. With a first-innings lead of 244 and virtually half the game left, it is difficult to imagine a more commanding position, particularly as we removed both openers by close of play. Yet the wicket is now playing very much more easily and it is plain that our task tomorrow may not be a formality by any means.

I chose to have the heavy roller on the pitch this morning and then, the decision made, gave the early-bird spectators another rare treat by indulging in a little batting practice against 'Giff'. So often, after a major stand such as Botham and Randall gave us yesterday, wickets fall quickly, but 'Beefy' was in a mood for further plundering. He launched a ferocious assault on the new ball and had moved rapidly to 138, of which 100 had come in boundaries, when he holed out wearily and gave Cairns his sixth wicket.

The big man's hopes of taking all ten were thwarted by Bob Taylor who, having looked in no trouble for forty-five minutes, set off for a speculative single with Randall on 99 and got himself run out. 'Arkle' spent an eternity stuck one short of three figures but when he finally broke the barrier he opened out quite dramatically. Meanwhile, Cairns removed Cook and Foster was given the treatment by Hadlee – a series of short balls which he negotiated, then one well up which he edged to third slip.

I made my entry in a helmet borrowed from Mike Gatting, who had taken to his bed suffering from a chest infection. I was soon glad I had taken the precaution. For reasons best known to himself Hadlee set about me with five bouncers in one seven-ball over. One of them crashed into my left temple and, but for the helmet, it could have been my lot. To my mind this was a pathetic piece of cricket by Hadlee. It is true that I dug one in at tailender Ewen Chatfield yesterday . . . but five in seven balls is taking vengeance a little far, especially as Hadlee had not run in at our early batsmen with anything like the same venom. I have said before he is a complicated mix as a cricketer; it now seems that may equally apply to his character. We contented ourselves with taking a silently dim view of the episode, which did in any case have its funny side. During the barrage I was attempting to employ the duck rather than the sway as evasive tactics, bearing in mind the occasion in 1982 when, again clad in a helmet, I had done a good deal of swaying against Imran Khan and consequently ricked my neck and missed a Test. In ducking rather rapidly, however, I succeeded in putting a twelve-inch split in the backside of my trousers. Dear old 'Flash' Cowans came to the rescue with a surprisingly nimble needle and thread during the tea interval.

'Arkle', who did not receive as many bouncers, battered his way brilliantly to 164 before being caught, thus leaving me undefeated for the fifty-second time in Tests. Is this another record?

I am delighted for Derek who remains a much criticized player and would not be in the England sides of many armchair critics. Over the years, however, he has been a tower of strength, uncomplaining no matter in what position he has had to bat. Perhaps now he is truly settled as a Test player.

Wright and Edgar opened aggressively for New Zealand, keen to reduce the deficit as rapidly as possible. But when I brought Cook into the attack, Wright played an impetuous shot and was caught at mid-on for the second time in the match. I was struggling for rhythm and bowling a lot of no-balls but, encouraged by Bob Taylor, I switched to bowling round the wicket against the left-handed Edgar. Soon, I found the edge, and Bob did the rest behind the stumps. Spurred on by success, I bowled two much more lively overs, but I am acutely aware that I am still lacking a yard of pace, rather like a horse who has been held up in training before a big race.

MONDAY 23 JANUARY Bernard Thomas phoned at 8.15 a.m. to report that Mike Gatting's temperature was still up. I said that if it was likely he could infect other people in the side he should not come to the ground. At breakfast, however, I talked through the options with A.C. and we decided that 'Gatt' was by some distance our best bat-pad fielder for the spinner, and that his gentle seamers might just be needed if we got stuck. So the decision was reversed, with the proviso that he report for duty an hour late, missing exercise and virtually stepping straight on to the field.

This was to be an interesting talking-point. I brought him on to bowl the last over before tea, when we had failed to take a single wicket in the session. He followed a rusty 'wide' by having Martin Crowe caught at slip for exactly 100. A.C. pointed out during the interval that we might well have decided to bring Mike to the

NEW ZEALAND 1ST INNINGS v. ENGLAND (1ST TEST) 1983-84 at BASIN RESERVE, WELLINGTON 20,21,22,23,24 JAN. TOSS: NEW ZEALAND

IN	OUT	MINS	No.	BATSMAN	HOW OUT	BOWLER	NOTES ON DISMISSAL	RUNS	WKT	TOTAL	6s	4s	BALLS
11.00	12.36	96	1	J.G.WRIGHT	c' COOK	BOTHAM	Misjudged line of hard successive bouncer - Mid-on catch.	17	1	34	.	1	82
11.00	12.45	105	2	B.A.EDGAR	c' TAYLOR	BOTHAM	Late on hook at short leg-side ball - faint edge.	9	2	39	.	.	72
12.39	2.03	44	3	G.P.HOWARTH *	c' GOWER	BOTHAM	Edged outswinger to gully - pushed forward.	15	3	56	.	1	35
12.47	2.33	66	4	M.D.CROWE	BOWLED	WILLIS	Misjudged line - attempted stroke too late - off bail down.	13	4	71	.	2	57
2.05	4.34	130	5	J.J.CROWE	c' TAYLOR	FOSTER	Edged off-drive at outswinger. HS in Tests	52	6	160	.	9	104
2.35	3.29	54	6	J.V.CONEY	c' GOWER	COOK	Edged flighted ball via pad to silly point.	27	5	114	.	4	46
3.31	5.09	79	7	R.J.HADLEE	c' GATTING	BOTHAM	Edged low to right of 2nd slip.	24	8	200	.	5	66
4.36	5.35	59	8	M.C.SNEDDEN	c' GATTING	WILLIS	Firm-footed push - edged to keeper (WILLIS 301ST WICKET)	11	7	174	.	2	41
5.11	11.08	57	9	I.D.S.SMITH †	LBW	BOTHAM	Played back and across breakback - kept low. HS in Tests.	24	10	219	.	3	45
5.37	5.51	14	10	B.L.CAIRNS	c' GATTING	WILLIS	Edged low to 3rd slip's right-diving 2-handed. WILLIS 308 WICKETS	3	9	208	.	.	12
5.53	(11.08)	15	11	E.J.CHATFIELD	NOT OUT			4			.	.	10
				EXTRAS	b 4 lb 9 w - nb 7			20			.	27⁴	
				TOTAL	(93.4 overs, 369 minutes)			219					570 balls (inc 8 no-balls) 2nd day

219 all out at 11.08 am 2nd day

* CAPTAIN † WICKET-KEEPER

BOWLER	O	M	R	W	nb		HRS	OVERS	RUNS
WILLIS	19	7	37	3	7		1	15	21
BOTHAM	27⁴	8	59	5	-		2	16	21
FOSTER	24	9	60	1	1		3	16	29
COOK	23	11	43	1	-		4	15	52
			20				5	17	51
	93.4	35	219	10			6	14	38

2ND NEW BALL taken at 5.29 pm on 1st day -
NEW ZEALAND 187-7 after 85 overs

RUNS	MINS	OVERS	LAST 50 (in mins)
50	132	33.1	132
100	213	53.1	81
150	257	65.5	44
200	334	86.1	77

LUNCH: 42-2
TEA: 123-5
STUMPS (1st DAY): 212-9

30 OVERS [120 MINUTES]	HOWARTH 7*	M.CROWE 1*
61 OVERS [241 MINUTES]	J.CROWE 34*	HADLEE 0*
92 OVERS [361 MINUTES]	SMITH 22*	CHATFIELD 0*

2ND DAY: NEW ZEALAND added 7 runs of 11 balls (including a no-ball) in 8 minutes.

BOTHAM took 5 wickets in an innings for the 21st time in Test Matches.

WKT	PARTNERSHIP		RUNS	MINS
1st	Wright	Edgar	34	96
2nd	Edgar	Howarth	5	6
3rd	Howarth	M.Crowe	17	36
4th	M.Crowe	J.Crowe	15	28
5th	J.Crowe	Coney	43	54
6th	J.Crowe	Hadlee	46	44
7th	Hadlee	Snedden	14	33
8th	Snedden	Smith	26	24
9th	Smith	Cairns	8	14
10th	Smith	Chatfield	11	15

15 OVERS 1 BALLS/HOUR
2.34 RUNS/OVER
38 RUNS/100 BALLS

219

© BILL FRINDALL 1984

ENGLAND 1st INNINGS   IN REPLY TO NEW ZEALAND'S 219 ALL OUT

IN	OUT	MINS	No.	BATSMAN	HOW OUT	BOWLER	RUNS	WKT	TOTAL	6s	4s	BALLS	NOTES ON DISMISSAL
11.20	12.43	83	1	C.J.TAVARÉ	BOWLED	CAIRNS	9	2	51	·	1	60	Played on - defensive back stroke rolled gently into stumps.
11.20	12.16	56	2	C.L.SMITH	c't HADLEE	CAIRNS	27	1	41	·	3	46	Edged drive to gully's left - diving 2-handed catch.
12.19	2.15	76	3	D.I.GOWER	c't HADLEE	CAIRNS	33	4	92	·	4	61	Brilliant right-handed mid-air catch at gully.
12.45	2.02	37	4	A.J.LAMB	c't M.D.CROWE	CAIRNS	13	3	84	·	2	36	Pushed forward - edged to square-leg's left hand. (catch above head)
2.04	2.49	45	5	M.W.GATTING	LBW	CAIRNS	19	5	115	·	3	39	Missed sweep.
2.17	11.32	235	6	I.T.BOTHAM	c't J.J.CROWE	CAIRNS	138	6	347	2	22	167	13th Test (3rd v NZ, 21st F.C.) Skied straight hit to square cover.
2.51	2.55	367	7	D.W.RANDALL	c't M.D.CROWE	HADLEE	164	10	463	2	20	270	6th in Tests (1st v NZ, 23rd F.C.) [50 min in 9½] Drove chest high to mid-wicket.
11.34	12.18	44	8	R.W.TAYLOR †	Run out (M.Crowe/Smith)		14	7	372	·	1	39	Randall attempted 100th run to square-leg. Close decision.
12.20	12.56	36	9	N.G.B.COOK	c't SMITH	CAIRNS	7	8	386	·	·	36	Edged firm-footed defensive push to wicket-keeper.
12.58	2.08	33	10	N.A.FOSTER	c't HOWARTH	HADLEE	10	9	426	·	2	30	Edged defensive push to 3rd slip - Howarth's 200th F.C catch.
2.10	(2.55)	45	11	R.G.D.WILLIS*	NOT OUT		5	·		·	·	32	52nd 'not out' - only batsman with 50 not outs in Tests.
				EXTRAS	b - lb 8	w - nb 16	24			4⁶	58⁴	816 balls (including 18 no balls)	

TOTAL (132.5 OVERS, 538 MINUTES) b - lb 8 w - nb 16 24

463 all out at 2.55 pm on 3rd day

ENGLAND'S HIGHEST TOTAL AT WELLINGTON (prev. 428.8A 1962-63)

*CAPTAIN †WICKET-KEEPER

14 OVERS 5 BALLS/HOUR
3.49 RUNS/OVER
57 RUNS/100 BALLS

RUNS	MINS	OVERS	LAST 50 (in mins)
50	72	16.3	72
100	148	36.2	76
150	198	48.3	50
200	251	61.4	53
250	295	71.3	44
300	348	86	53
350	379	93.3	31
400	468	116.4	89
450	520	129.1	52

ENGLAND LEAD: 244 RUNS

BOWLER	O	M	R	W	nb	HRS	OVERS	RUNS
HADLEE	31.5	6	97	2	13	1	14	45
SNEDDEN	21	3	101	0	2	2	15	38
CAIRNS	45	10	143	7		3	15	42
CHATFIELD	28	6	68	0	3	4	15	60
M.D.CROWE	3	0	20	0		5	14	70
CONEY	4	1	10	0		6	16	62
			24	1		7	15	55
	132.5	26	463	10		8	16	44

2ND NEW BALL taken at 11.04am 3rd day
- ENGLAND 295-5 after 85 overs

LUNCH: 62-2	GOWER 13* (42) LAMB 6* (16)	24 OVERS	101 MIN
TEA: 172-5	BOTHAM 42* (83) RANDALL 17* (49)	54 OVERS	220 MIN
STUMPS: 293-5 (2ND DAY)	BOTHAM 105* (203) RANDALL 71* (169)	84 OVERS	340 MIN
LUNCH: 394-8	RANDALL 150* (292) FOSTER 4* (5')	115 OVERS	463 MIN

BOTHAM: 100 & 5 WKTS IN TEST INNINGS FOR 5TH TIME (record)

ENGLAND'S RECORD SIXTH-WICKET PARTNERSHIP AGAINST ALL COUNTRIES IS 240 BY P.H.PARFITT AND B.R.KNIGHT v NZ AT AUCKLAND 1962-63.

RANDALL'S SCORE OF 164 IS THE HIGHEST IN NZ v E TESTS AT WELLINGTON (prev. 136 - C.S.DEMPSTER 1929)

WKT	PARTNERSHIP		RUNS	MINS
1st	Tavaré	Smith	41	56
2nd	Tavaré	Gower	10	24
3rd	Gower	Lamb	33	37
4th	Gower	Gatting	8	11
5th	Gatting	Botham	23	32
6th	Botham	Randall	232	201
7th	Randall	Taylor	25	44
8th	Randall	Cook	14	36
9th	Randall	Foster	40	33
10th	Randall	Willis	37	45
			463	

© BILL FRINDALL 1984

NEW ZEALAND 2ND INNINGS   244 RUNS BEHIND ON FIRST INNINGS

IN	OUT	MINS	No.	BATSMAN	HOW OUT	BOWLER	RUNS	WKT	TOTAL	6s	4s	BALLS	NOTES ON DISMISSAL
3·08	4·51	85	1	J.G.WRIGHT	c FOSTER	COOK	35	1	62	·	3	69	Miscued. Lofted on drive - chest high to mid-on.
3·08	5·22	116	2	B.A.EDGAR	c TAYLOR	WILLIS	30	2	79	·	3	85	Edged offside ball, bowled from round the wicket.
4·54	12·00	126	3	G.P.HOWARTH*	Run out (COOK)		34	3	153	·	5	90	Bowler deflected straight drive from M.D.Crowe into stumps.
5·24	3·40	278	4	M.D.CROWE	c BOTHAM	GATTING	100	5	279	·	19	245	Edged outswinger to slip. (1st in Tests. (11th f-c. GATTING's 19 Test wkt.
12·03	12·20	17	5	J.J.CROWE	LBW	BOTHAM	3	4	165	·	·	16	Played back to full length ball after two successive bouncers.
12·22 (3·41)	3·41	490	6	J.V.CONEY	NOT OUT		174			1	26	373	(1st in Test. (5th f-c. (11th since 1977). HS - ENGLAND by NZ in home Test. HS (f-c)
4·00	4·21	21	7	R.J.HADLEE	c LAMB	FOSTER	18	6	302	·	3	19	Cut short ball high to gully - leaping right-handed catch.
4·23	5·16	53	8	M.C.SNEDDEN	c TAYLOR	FOSTER	16	7	334	·	2	44	Edged inswing/in away-seamer.
5·18	12·57	108	9	I.D.S.SMITH †	BOWLED	COOK	29	8	402	·	3	81	Leg stump - missed sweep at leg-break. HS in Tests.
12·39	3·30	131	10	B.L.CAIRNS	c SUB (G.FOWLER)	WILLIS	64	9	520	1	11	114	Drove chest high to cover. HS in Tests. (WILLIS's 310th wkt)
3·30	3·41	11	11	E.J.CHATFIELD	BOWLED	COOK	0	10	537	·	·	7	Bowled behind legs attempting a sweep.
				EXTRAS	b 4 lb 14	w 2 nb 14	34			2b	75b	11143 balls (inc. 19 no balls × 1 5-ball over)	
				TOTAL	(187·3 overs, 726 MINUTES)		537						all out at 3·41 pm on 5th day.

* CAPTAIN   † WICKET-KEEPER

15 OVERS 3 BALLS/HOUR
2·86 RUNS/OVER
47 RUNS/100 BALLS

HRS	OVERS	RUNS
1	15	48
2	13	31
3	16	39
4	16	51
5	18	29
6	15	53
7	14	56
8	14	28
9	16	27
10	16	57
11	17	46

BOWLER	O	M	R	W	
WILLIS	37	8	102	2	17½
BOTHAM	36	6	137	2	-
FOSTER	37	12	91	2	·
COOK	66·3	26	153	3	3½
GATTING	8	4	14	1	1½
SMITH	3	1	6	0	-
	187·3	57	537	10	

2ND NEW BALL taken at 2·30 pm 4th day) - NEW ZEALAND 227-4 after 85 overs.
3RD NEW BALL taken 2·35 pm 5th day) ... NZ 445-8 after 170 overs.

NEW ZEALAND'S HIGHEST TOTAL IN NEW ZEALAND AND HIGHEST BY ANY COUNTRY AT WELLINGTON.

	RUNS	MINS	OVERS	LAST 50 (in mins)
	50	63	15·4	63
	100	159	38·3	96
	150	214	53·2	55
	200	300	78·2	86
	250	356	91·5	56
	300	412	105·4	56
	350	518	130·3	106
	400	575	145·3	57
	450	650	167·2	75
	500	701	180·2	51

TEA: 26-0 [8 OVERS 34 MIN] — WRIGHT 19* EDGAR 5*

STUMPS: 93-2 (3RD DAY) [37 OVERS 154 MIN] NZ 151 BEHIND — HOWARTH 11* (46) M.CROWE 8* (36)

LUNCH: 191-4 [71 OVERS 277 MIN] — M.CROWE 57* (58) CONEY 16* (41)

TEA: 279-5 [101·3 OVERS 396 MIN] — CONEY 55* (160)

STUMPS: 335-7 (4TH DAY) [122·2 OVERS 485 MIN] (31 MIN LOST) 35 AHEAD — CONEY 76* (248) SMITH 1* (11)

LUNCH: 419-8 [153 OVERS 605 MIN] — CONEY 114* (369) CAIRNS 13* (21)

† RECORD NZ 9th WICKET record against all countries.

WKT	PARTNERSHIP		RUNS	MINS
1st	Wright	Edgar	62	85
2nd	Edgar	Howarth	17	28
3rd	Howarth	M.Crowe	74	96
4th	M.Crowe	J.Crowe	12	17
5th	M.Crowe	Coney	114	160
6th	Coney	Hadlee	23	21
7th	Coney	Snedden	32	53
8th	Coney	Smith	68	108
9th	Coney	Cairns	118†	131
10th	Coney	Chatfield	17	11
			537	

© BILL FRINDALL 1984

ENGLAND 2ND INNINGS   NEEDING 294 RUNS TO WIN IN A MINIMUM OF 117 MINUTES

IN	OUT	MINS	No.	BATSMAN	HOW OUT	BOWLER	RUNS	WKT TOTAL	6s	4s	BALLS	NOTES ON DISMISSAL
4.03	(5.30)	87	1	C.J. TAVARÉ	NOT OUT		36		.	3	75	
4.03	(5.30)	87	2	C.L. SMITH	NOT OUT		30		.	4	60	
			3	D.I. GOWER								
			4	A.J. LAMB								
			5	M.W. GATTING								
			6	I.T. BOTHAM								
			7	D.W. RANDALL	DID NOT BAT							
			8	R.W. TAYLOR †								
			9	N.G.B. COOK								
			10	N.A. FOSTER								
			11	R.G.D. WILLIS *								
				EXTRAS	b - lb - w - nb 3		3		-	7	135 balls (inc. 3 no balls)	
				TOTAL	(22 OVERS, 87 MINUTES)			69-0				

* CAPTAIN   † WICKET-KEEPER

BOWLER	O	M	R	W	nb		HRS	OVERS	RUNS		RUNS	MINS	OVERS	LAST 50 (in mins)
SNEDDEN	7	2	28	0	3		1	13	58		50	52	12	52
CHATFIELD	5	0	24	0	-									
M.D. CROWE	6	1	11	0	-									
EDGAR	3	0	3	0	-									
J.J. CROWE	1	1	0	0										
					3									
	22	5	69	0										

15 OVERS 1 BALLS/HOUR
3.14 RUNS/OVER
51 RUNS/100 BALLS

WKT	PARTNERSHIP		RUNS	MINS
1st	Tavaré	Smith	69*	87

MATCH DRAWN

PLAY ABANDONED at 5.30pm 5th day after 9 of 20 overs mandatory in final hour.

TOTAL ATTENDANCE: 30,000

GATE RECEIPTS: $NZ 82,300 (£38,143.80)

TOTAL TIME LOST: 31 MINUTES

MAN OF THE MATCH: I.T. BOTHAM

© BILL FRINDALL 1984

ground at lunchtime, in which event he would not have been able to bowl until after tea. Even now, that wicket he took could be decisive, for New Zealand ended the day on 335 – in effect 91 – for seven and, although our progress was sometimes slow today, we should still force home our advantage, given decent weather tomorrow.

The pitch has now lost all its spite and today's plan depended greatly on Nick Cook's ability to block up an end, bowling his spinners into the wind while the faster bowlers rotated from the more favourable end. This, I'm afraid, he did not manage at all successfully. His bowling lacked rhythm and consistency and he failed to take a wicket all day.

We had two good spells, the first of these coming early on when Howarth was unluckily run out while backing up as Crowe's drive deflected on to the non-striker's stumps off Cook's outstretched fingers; and then twenty minutes later Jeff Crowe was lbw to Ian. The younger Crowe, however, was soon playing shots. He has been compared to Greg Chappell and it is not difficult to appreciate why when he bats like this. Interestingly, though, his Test average before today was a mere 17. It is a good bit more now after a fine maiden Test century during which he played and missed at nothing.

Our other good period came at the end of the day when Foster summoned the energy for a fine spell which produced two wickets, those of Hadlee and Snedden, and could have brought more. Neil continues to impress me greatly, both with his bowling and his general attitude. For one so young he has shown himself able and willing to do the grafting as well as seeking the glory.

The last session was disrupted by bad light, which left us fretting in frustration. But although the four-day win which once seemed a good possibility has not transpired, I still feel we ought to finish the job tomorrow.

We laughed again tonight over the type of incident which appeals to the humour of all cricketers except the poor guy involved. David Gower had come to me during the afternoon saying he felt rough and might have to go off. He returned temporarily to his position at third slip but, midway through the next over, retreated rapidly – but too late – with his hand thrown to his mouth. He blamed the fruit salad we had for lunch . . .

TUESDAY 24 JANUARY The one that got away . . . and I suppose we may live to rue it. Briefly, New Zealand's tailenders hung around with the superb Jerry Coney long enough to put the game beyond us – and moral victories count for nothing in Test cricket.

Their innings occupied a little over two full days' play and their final total of 537 reflects great credit on the new spirit of resolve in the Kiwi side. Maybe it also reflects the fact that we still lack penetration, but in truth the ball was barely rising above stump height today. Our prognosis that the pitch would not improve for batting turned out to be wide of the mark and by the end of the game it needed unforced errors to bring wickets.

Coney was magnificent. He has been an unsung hero of New Zealand's recent improvement and perhaps this innings will bring him some of the acclaim he deserves. He batted more than eight hours, remaining unbeaten on 174, and the way he kept the tailenders going was as striking as his own batting.

It was a bad day from the start. My match-morning existence shies away from disruption and I was disturbed that I had to wait half an hour for toast and coffee in the breakfast-room due to an enormous influx of racing folk heading for the horse sales. It set the pace for the day – we spent an awful long time waiting vainly for wickets to fall. I tried as many permutations as I had available but the options were limited, with Cook still below his best and Botham suffering from a muscle strain in his backside.

The equation is confusing: on good pitches we need five bowlers but on bad pitches we need seven batsmen. This pitch played better than we expected, but the selection problem is likely to stay with us either until we find another all-rounder or until Bob Taylor's eventual retirement brings in a batting wicket-keeper.

Disappointment was obvious tonight after we had come so close, only to fail with the killer punch. But, on reflection, the game had a number of plusses for us in view of the very limited preparation. Botham was one, Randall another, Foster certainly a third. We have something to build on and should be encouraged rather than downhearted by this performance.

Went to a party tonight and probably drank too much red wine.

4

CARNAGE
AT CHRISTCHURCH

WEDNESDAY 25 JANUARY 'Arkle' was sick on the plane this morning.
That makes four so far to have gone down with whatever mild bug
is doing the rounds. Like the other three, D. Randall expected and
received his quota of mickey-taking for falling victim to a pheno-
menon which invariably causes great mirth to all except the person
involved.

The trip from Wellington to Dunedin, New Zealand's Scottish
capital, took two hours by air, but Ian Botham had requested and
been permitted to do it by ferry and car – a distance of some six
hundred miles by road which he broke up by indulging in his
passion for fishing. He arrived in the hotel late tonight, brandishing
the spoils of his efforts.

I had spent the afternoon catching up on some reading and some
sleep, in that order, and then spent the evening at the local trotting
meeting. I have never been surprised that this sport has failed to
catch on in the UK. For those who have not seen it, the racehorses
pull their jockeys who are seated on a two-wheeled affair called a
'sulky' wielding an oversized whip. It is very big in the Antipodes
but, for my money, is not a patch on proper racing as an entertainment. Dunedin not being too big on entertainment, however,
tonight it provided a pleasant enough diversion, although I was
happy to have arrived late as my five bets were all unplaced.

The day was completely free from cricket and made an enjoyable
break. Tomorrow we must get back to work.

THURSDAY 26 JANUARY Neil Foster has become an established part
of the early breakfast team which has, for some tours now, featured
Bob Taylor, Chris Tavaré and myself. 'Fozzy' is a welcome addition, seldom being short of something enlivening to say, and this
morning he was regaling us with some remarkable tales of the
goings-on at a local golf course yesterday. Norman Cowans, it
seems, is not one to abide by the etiquette of the Royal and Ancient,

even if he is familiar with it. 'Fozzy' reports that everyone in sight was in fear of his life whenever 'Flash' wielded his driver on the fairway, and that he was once seen taking a seven-iron on the green! I make no claims to being a golfer, but even I raised my eyebrows and spluttered on my brown toast over that.

We are due to meet Otago here tomorrow. With two months of the tour still to run, it is amazing that this will be our final three-day match. One can only pity those whose form does not merit selection for the next Test, as they will have to rely almost solely on the inadequacies of others to get their places back.

Otago used to play on the Carisbrook rugby ground. Their temporary cricket base, where we practised today, is a great improvement – especially aesthetically. It is green, pleasant and tree-lined, and on a sunny day like today it was a pleasure to be there. We practised, without the still-suffering Botham, for just over an hour and then, having decided on tomorrow's line-up, a number of us departed for an afternoon outing.

The temperature had risen into the eighties as we drove down the Otago Peninsular, watched seals and penguins basking in the sun and then paid a visit to the Royal Albatross Colony at Tairoa Head. It is apparently the only colony of its type built within the boundaries of a city and those in charge go to a lot of trouble to ensure the birds are not pestered or frightened. With their huge heads, and wingspans of about ten feet, they are an incredible sight and I was very glad I had made the effort to come and see them.

A splendid day ended at a French restaurant just across the road from the hotel where we had the best meal I have eaten in New Zealand. The company included Graeme Fowler and Graham Dilley, both of whom have matured quite noticeably since their last overseas trip. 'Foxy' said tonight that he had found last winter's Australian tour long, arduous and rather strange, but felt better adjusted to this one. 'Picca', who had a tendency to sulk in the past if things were not going his way, is now a much more positive bloke. He admits going through a spell when he was content to sit on his backside and get away with doing as little as possible but says he is now determined he won't be carrying the drinks again and willing to work as hard as is necessary to hold down a place in the side. I left the restaurant thinking how refreshing it was to hear such statements from members of a generation whose attitudes to work I have often questioned.

FRIDAY 27 JANUARY On a tour of New Zealand one must tolerate some bad weather, but when the rain comes to disrupt a playing schedule as narrow as this one, frustration is inevitable. With so little cricket between the Tests, we need every available opportunity to get people in form. Losing an entire day, as we did today, is close to being a disaster.

It was coming down in stair-rods when I peered out of my window at 7.15 this morning and it didn't stop until four in the afternoon. By that time all chance of any play had been literally washed away.

We stayed in the hotel until after eleven, there being no point in sitting unprofitably at the ground, but eventually we organized some indoor training at a centre just down the road from the ground. We did our usual stretching exercises there and some of the lads played tennis.

Watched a science-fiction movie called *Krull* to pass the afternoon. It was dreadful, but on a wet Friday in Dunedin there is precious little choice.

SATURDAY 28 JANUARY There were no interruptions today but plenty more frustrations. Under clear skies and on a presentable pitch, our batsmen threw away the chance of a confidence-boosting innings. I ended the day concerned about our durability and about the progress we are making as a team.

The ground had dried well, I noticed, when I arrived from an official champagne breakfast given by the local cricket association. As I was not playing, David Gower went out for the toss. He won it and we batted – poorly.

Chris Tavaré's early dismissal was perhaps the most worrying feature of the day. When he is in form he is the rock around which our strokemakers can play, but recently he has not looked the part at all and I detect signs that he is getting down in the dumps about it. 'Kippy' Smith's fallibility against the short ball was again apparent, Allan Lamb played across a half-volley, the other leading batsmen followed equally tamely and it was quickly down to messrs Taylor and Marks to get us out of an embarrassing hole and into a position of respect. We were eventually able to declare at tea with eight wickets down, but then the rain came back to haunt us, cutting our session in the field down to an hour, during which both Cowans and Dilley looked rusty through lack of bowling.

At the end of play I had a serious word with the team about our batting performance, stressing that I was disappointed at the apparent lack of concentration and application. I feel now that I have to hammer away at them on this subject because time is so short before what may well be a crucial Second Test. We have been hearing horror stories about the Christchurch wicket for weeks now, and if it is half as bad as rumour would have it, there is sure to be a result. If we get on the wrong end of it, the series may be as good as lost.

Had dinner tonight with A.C. and Bob Taylor . . . three old pros chatting about old-fashioned ideals and bemoaning the lack of professionalism apparent in certain of the younger generation. It at least got it off our chests.

Back at the hotel I ran into 'Beefy', who gave me his own impressions of the highs and lows being experienced by certain individuals on the trip. It was valuable to hear a detached view.

SUNDAY 29 JANUARY The match with Otago subsided peacefully and inevitably into a draw, while off the field we counted our walking wounded like a battalion at war. This morning, when I woke, our only fitness worry was the strain still affecting Ian. By tonight the list included our only specialist wicket-keeper and four of our five seam bowlers – surprisingly, I am the only one who still has nothing to complain about.

Bob Taylor reported at breakfast that his groin, which he had twisted while keeping wicket yesterday, had become very sore overnight. It was decided he should rest today and Fowler took over the gloves.

Our next and most major problem occurred at nets, yours truly cast as the unwitting villain of the piece. I had been bowling for some while off my short run, fearful of coming in properly because the footholds were still wet. Neil Foster went in to bat and, towards the end of his knock, I bowled him a yorker on middle-and-leg stump. In trying to keep it out, he jammed his bat hard against the inside of his front foot, while the ball pitched full toss on his little toe. He yelped in pain and went rapidly to hospital, where a cracked bone was confirmed. He is very sore and will almost certainly be out for about ten days, missing at least the Second and maybe even the Third Test.

As if this was not enough to cast a pall of depression over everyone, Graham Dilley reported he was suffering from blisters on his heel, which may seem a minor ailment but is painful for a quick bowler; and Norman Cowans joined Taylor in the groin-strain brigade. All in all, it was a sorry picture and left me in thoughtful mood as I departed by road for Alexandra with an advance party of A.C. Smith and Foster.

I was still, however, aware of the fascinating changes in scenery during the drive from coastal to central Otago. We passed from verdant greens to an altogether starker landscape, we saw snow on the hills and then finally we arrived in what is a very prosperous fruit-growing area with a warm, dry climate. They have only ten inches of rain each year here, so I hope they don't use up any of that ration to spoil our one-day fixture tomorrow.

ENGLAND v OTAGO

Played at University Oval, Dunedin, 27, 28, 29 Jan 1984

Drawn

ENGLAND XI 194 for 8 dec (V. J. Marks 50, N. A. Mallender 4 for 53) and 118 for 4

OTAGO 152 for 9 dec (K. R. Rutherford 47, V. J. Marks 5 for 52)

MONDAY 30 JANUARY Bernard told me at breakfast that he considered Cowans and Dilley fit to play today but not Foster, Taylor and Botham. This immediately reduced us to a twelve-man squad and the news grew more worrying when Bob Taylor reported that he had hardly slept a wink for the discomfort of his injury. With the Test four days away, this is cause for serious concern and I suggested to A.C. that we should line up a replacement wicket-keeper. Later today he phoned Donald Carr at Lord's with the request that Paul Downton, of Middlesex, be alerted to fly here at short notice from Stellenbosch, in South Africa, where he is spending the winter. His journey will apparently take all of forty-eight hours, so we will have to make a decision tomorrow. We took a calculated risk when we chose only one keeper for this tour and were always aware that 'Chat' could break down just before a Test. At the very worst, Graeme Fowler can keep wicket in the Test. I hope it doesn't come to that.

I picked up a copy of the local morning paper from the reception area in our motel and read that the New Zealand selectors had called up the left-arm spinner Stephen Boock and replaced Martin Snedden with another seamer in Derek Stirling. This would seem a sound move as Stirling was lively and consistent when he bowled against us at Palmerston North.

Before leaving for the ground I had to borrow some shaving kit and a toothbrush, having left mine in Dunedin yesterday. I hope somebody sends them on – I don't feel at my best with whiskers and can't go on borrowing razors.

We won our game against Otago Invitation XI easily enough. Their captain Warren Lees wanted us to bat first in case his side collapsed quickly in front of the big crowd. We obliged him in that respect, but also put the match out of their reach by scoring 297 in 50 overs. 'Tav' and 'Lego' were among the runs, which will do both of them some good, but it was a pity neither Gatting nor Randall had much opportunity for a decent knock.

Our bowling and fielding had a lethargic look. It was a slow pitch, and every time Cowans dropped the ball short he was hit for four. Dilley had run-up troubles so we were not altogether impressive. But we still had plenty of runs in the bank and, once the required rate rose above eight an over, some of the Otago guys looked to be playing for themselves.

After play, a bus took us to a lakeside hotel in Queenstown, where we are spending the night prior to flying on to our Test base in Christchurch. The drive of an hour or so took us through picturesque scenery, decanting us at the sort of idyllic spot I would love to linger at if we did not have cricket on our minds.

ENGLAND XI v OTAGO INVITATION XI

Played at Molyneux Park, Alexandra, 30 Jan 1984

England XI won by 112 runs

ENGLAND XI 297 for 4 in 50 overs (C. J. Tavaré 126, A. J. Lamb 106 not out)

OTAGO 185 for 8 in 50 overs (S. J. McCullum 97 not out, B. R. Blair 53)

TUESDAY 31 JANUARY With some trepidation, I kept a breakfast appointment with A.C., Norman Gifford, Bernard Thomas and the cause of our anxiety, Bob Taylor. I had ordered my toast and coffee by the time the others arrived, and the sight of Bob's altogether cheerier expression told me all would be well. He said he felt one hundred per cent better than yesterday and Bernard assured us that the improvement should now be fairly rapid. So, confident that Bob will be OK for Friday, we cancelled the alert to Paul Downton. It is a great relief, because Paul would have arrived here barely twenty-four hours before the game, not the best of preparations for a Test.

With half the day to wile away before our flight to Christchurch, I sat out on the hotel balcony, reading my book and intermittently drinking in the spectacular view across Lake Wakatipu. There was a mist rolling down from the mountains, while light aircraft and helicopters hurried past and, down on the water, small craft ferried tourists to the areas designated for jetboating and white-water rafting. Some of our lads had gone off in search of such lively activities, but they did not appeal to me. Instead, putting my book away at midday, I wandered the half-mile into the small town, met some of the travelling press and joined them on board an old steamer, the SS *Earnslaw*, for a gentle cruise across the lake.

I grabbed a pizza lunch, the adventurous guys regaling me with hairy accounts of their rafting in the rapids, then returned to base prior to our short but spectacular flight over Mount Cook to Christchurch.

Among the other guests in the Chateau Regency Hotel are The Shadows, who seem to have been around all my life at least. I bumped into their manager who kindly asked if any of our lads would like to go to their concert tonight. Up in the team-room I rounded up some eager volunteers in the shapes of messrs Foster, Cowans and Randall.

I had a previous booking for dinner with David Heard, our liaison man here. I met him on the previous full tour to New Zealand six years ago and we have been friends ever since. He writes to me and occasionally, despite my shortcomings in that department, gets a letter back. On tour he is a marvel: nothing is too much trouble for him and tonight's dinner was just one example of his hospitality. Peter Smith of the *Daily Mail* and Pat Gibson of the *Express* were also present and we chatted generally about the apparent shortcomings of New Zealand's cricket administration and the possibility that they may miss out on the benefits of the current explosion of interest unless they change their ways.

WEDNESDAY I FEBRUARY Juliet phoned to tell me she is going into hospital to have the baby. This is earlier than expected but there are apparently no reasons for alarm. I reassured her as best I could that all was well with me. At this distance all I can do is hope there are no problems and wait for news.

My first view of the notorious Christchurch wicket did not do much to allay the natural fears. I looked at it on my way across the ground to the nets area and, although it was not quite the horrific sight the adverse publicity would have had us believe, it was certainly very rough in areas. But I have been unwisely drawn on previous occasions into making premature comments about the state of a pitch. This time I shall keep quiet.

Of the two practice areas available, one was in the sun, the other in the shade and on a damp surface. We opted for the hot, dry area and I bowled for forty-five minutes off my long run, feeling quite good. 'Picca', however, is in a lot of trouble with his run-up and rhythm and looks to be getting down about it. I told him that I have many times experienced similar problems and the worst thing one can do is take the negative attitude and mope about it.

Paid another visit to a stud farm this afternoon in the customary company of 'Giff' and 'Beefy'. This one was rather different as they specialize in breeding horses for trotting through an artificial insemination process. Having watched the entire routine with great fascination, the three of us each pulled the trigger for an injection of semen into a mare. We came back and told the lads that we had each covered a mare. Some of them looked bemused . . .

This evening was an abstemious one. I drank water in the bar and 'Beefy' and I agreed we would not eat anything. Already, I have cut down from English to continental breakfast but I still feel I am eating too much.

John Snow arrived in the hotel with a fresh party of supporters. There are now more than a hundred folk here from England so we should have a noticeable contingent behind us on Friday.

THURSDAY 2 FEBRUARY Our fractured, anxious build-up to this Test finally reached crisis point today and we had to resort to finding a replacement seam bowler. At the height of the negotiations, I learned that I am the father of a healthy daughter. For a time, everything else seemed suddenly unimportant, but this was such a frantic pre-Test day that I had regrettably few minutes to dwell on it.

It was A.C. who broke the news. I had just returned from a courtesy visit to the company supplying our cars here when the manager appeared at my door, demanding to know how long I had been back. When I said 'five seconds' he looked relieved and congratulated me on the arrival. Everything is evidently well with Juliet and the baby, although delivery was induced. I wanted to phone, of course, but A.C. told me that Juliet was under sedation and I would have to wait until tomorrow.

No sooner had the news sunk in than I had to drag my thoughts back to cricket for our evening tactical team meeting – but before we began, A.C. insisted that everyone should have a sip of champagne.

Our team discussions were complicated by yet more developments in the injury saga. We were pretty much resigned to being without Foster and, although he put on his boots and tried to run in at this morning's net practice, six painful deliveries were enough to confirm him a non-runner. The alarm bells rang, though, when it became clear that Dilley had strained his thigh rather more seriously than anyone imagined. He struggled badly this morning and looks in grave doubt. With some concern still being expressed over Cowans's groin, we plainly needed to make rapid contingency plans so I cut short my own net session and entered into discussions over possible recuits.

We knew that two likely lads were already in the country – Neil Mallender of Northants and Tony Pigott of Sussex. With the notice so short, the choice seemed to rest between them and, as I had seen Pigott bowl only once in three years, I consulted the other selectors for their views and also talked to Allan Lamb, who would naturally know more about his county team-mate Mallender than anyone else. I received some conflicting opinions but when David Gower and Norman Gifford joined the discussion they came down strongly on the side of Pigott and I was swayed by their conviction.

'Lester', as he is rather obviously known, was, we discovered, finishing a three-day game against Central Districts at Palmerston North. That, in itself, was no problem – he could still be on a flight to Christchurch in plenty of time. His more pressing personal dilemma was that we had dropped a bombshell on his wedding plans. He and his fiancé Nicky had planned to get married next Monday but, putting his career first, he has agreed to postpone the date. Under the circumstances, we agreed that he could bring Nicky with him. He was quickly on a flight here, stopping off at Wellington to pick up some clothes, and A.C. and I went to meet him this evening, trying hard to make him feel as much at home as is possible in the brief time available. He may yet not be needed, if we feel a spinner might be useful, but I think the chances are he will be in the side, and his wedding will have to wait.

The remainder of our team selection had been much less complex: Fowler took the second opener's place ahead of Smith; Gatting held on to his middle-order position despite having done little to dispel the doubts about his ability at the highest level; and Vic Marks was brought into the squad instead of Nick Cook, who bowled so disappointingly in Wellington. The selection meeting had not taken long and neither had the press conference, as the journalists fell so hungrily on the Pigott story that they seemed not to worry about anything else. I said little to them about the wicket – it is obviously giving us some worries but it is all too easy to have team confidence undermined by doomy predictions on the behaviour of a pitch and I am determined to avoid that.

What with one thing and another it was pushing 11 p.m. when I got to bed, later than my usual hour for the night prior to a Test.

FRIDAY 3 FEBRUARY I telephoned Juliet in hospital just before eight, got through without difficulty and was delighted to hear all is well with them both. It was just about the only thing to go right all day.

After a swift breakfast I took 'Picca' to the ground to test his thigh. We set off more in hope than confidence and it was obvious after eight balls that he was nowhere near fit enough to contemplate a five-day Test. So we were down to twelve men, the final place resting between 'Lester' and the spinner. The doubt was swiftly resolved, for when we met on the pitch and fingered the cracks, the selectors unanimously agreed we should play all four seamers, on the basis that the slower bowlers would be easier to play against even if the ball did turn. So poor 'Skid' missed out again and A.C.S. Pigott, an unlikely Old Harrovian, was to make a dramatic and totally unexpected Test début.

We badly wanted to bat first, as there seems no chance of conditions improving, but for the second time in two Tests my call of 'tails' was wrong and Geoff Howarth inevitably elected to take first knock. Back in the dressing-room, I stressed to the guys how important a day lay ahead and that we must make things go our way despite the loss of a toss I, privately, considered might be crucial. For a while, things went pretty much to plan. Wright and Edgar enjoyed some early good fortune against me and, although Ian bowled poorly with the new ball, 'Lester' kept to the script of his personal fairy story with a wicket in his second over, Edgar being caught round the corner.

Cowans picked up two wickets, having Wright caught behind and then bowling Howarth, and when Martin Crowe was magnificently caught at slip by Chris Tavaré, the Kiwis were 87 for four and we were in a commanding position despite not being at our best.

My lunchtime lecture pulled no punches, telling the lads we had bowled rubbish and that we must improve line and length. But it seemed to have the opposite effect. The afternoon was a nightmare as Jeff Crowe and Coney got stuck into us and then, when Crowe fell leg-before to Cowans, Hadlee came in to play the type of innings he produces so regularly against us.

We just could not bowl to him, and it was then that we really missed Neil Foster. At Wellington, 'Fozzy' had bowled so well to Hadlee that he earned himself a few bouncers in frustrated return, and this pitch would undoubtedly have suited his style. Instead, we had Ian bowling dreadfully, 'Lester' being slogged quite fearfully after an enouraging start and me resorting to my Sunday League run-up because I was finding I had very little body action off my full approach.

I bowled with better control off the short run and took four of the last five wickets, including the satisfying scalp of Hadlee on 99. But satisfaction was strictly rationed, because it all came far too late. New Zealand totalled 307 – utterly ridiculous in these conditions, but an accurate reflection of the bowling. The decision to play four seamers was absolutely right but was taken without the knowledge that we would bowl like mugs.

Ian Botham was unbelievably bad – right back to his worst days of last winter in Australia. He had no rhythm or speed in his run-up and no direction with the ball when he got there. After his marvellous performance in Wellington, this was a particularly bitter pill to

The Basin Reserve, Wellington, one of the most picturesque cricket grounds
in the world and venue for the First Test against New Zealand.

ABOVE Friend and longstanding colleague Ian Botham – whose contribution to the First Test was five wickets in an innings for the twenty-first time in Tests and a swashbuckling century – shares my moment of glory as I become England's leading wicket-taker. *John Selkirk/The Dominion and NZ Times*

LEFT Richard Hadlee's response to my digging one in at tailender Ewen Chatfield. Five bouncers – including one that struck me on the temple – in a seven-ball over was, I believe, taking vengeance little far.

LEFT Chris Tavaré, so often the sheet-anchor for England but sadly lacking during this particular tour, at nets prior to the Christchurch Test.

RIGHT The England bowling performance on the first day at Christchurch was the worst I can recall and the prime reason for us losing the match. Richard Hadlee exploited our weaknesses to the full by plundering us for 99 off 81 balls.

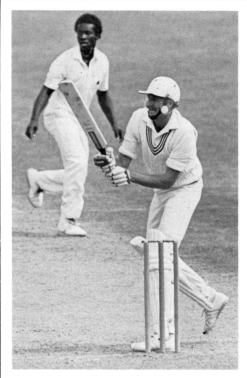

ABOVE LEFT Jeremy Coney, the unsung hero of New Zealand's recent improvement, who followed up 174 not out in the First Test with an important 41 in the Second, thus helping to set up New Zealand's quickest and largest-ever Test victory.

ABOVE RIGHT One of the wickets to fall during our spineless display of batting at Christchurch: Allan Lamb, caught behind off Chatfield.

LEFT Tony Pigott, emergency stand-in for the injured Foster and Dilley, dutifully postponed his wedding which was scheduled for the fourth day of play – only to find that the game ended on the third day.

ABOVE Manager Alan Smith, myself and assistant-manager Norman Gifford at a practice session after the débâcle at Christchurch – no doubt wondering how we were going to avoid England's first ever series defeat against New Zealand.

BELOW LEFT Ian Botham exercising during the Third Test at Auckland, suffering the effects of his long-term knee injury which was to force him home early from Pakistan.

BELOW RIGHT John Wright and Jeff Crowe, whose centuries in New Zealand's first innings ensured that the Third Test would end in stalemate.

ABOVE Ian Smith – man of
the match in the Third Test –
watches Chris Smith on his way
to top-scoring for England in the
second one-day international. By
a strange coincidence, the two
Smiths headed their country's
Test batting averages.

LEFT Much missed during the
Christchurch Test, Neil Foster
played a vital role, full of
maturity, in our victory in the
first one-day international.

OPPOSITE

ABOVE LEFT Vic Marks, who had
New Zealand reeling in the
second one-day international
with figures of five for 20.

ABOVE RIGHT Martin Crowe,
whose maiden Test century at
Wellington and match-winning
century in the third one-day
international prompted people to
compare him with Greg Chappell

BELOW LEFT My old mate Geoff
Howarth directing traffic during
the one-day internationals.

BELOW RIGHT Elton John, whose
three concerts in the same town
as the one-day internationals
were a great send-off to quieter
times in Pakistan.

A lot went wrong in New Zealand but nobody could have any complaints about the performances of Derek Randall – a century against Northern Districts, two Test centuries and then the man of the match award in the first one-day game.

swallow, for at his best he could have wrecked the Kiwi innings today.

The last straw in a dreadful day came with the loss of Fowler at a minute to six, and I must say it was difficult for a natural pessimist like myself to look on the bright side this evening. I tried to console myself that I was wrong in Wellington, where I had considered our 463 to be a winning score, and I might be wrong again here. But I could not get away from the plain fact that this match is going to produce a result unless the weather intervenes pretty severely – and we are going to be on the wrong end of that result unless we can bat a great deal more professionally than we bowled.

There seemed no real point in inquests or rollickings tonight. Everyone needs lifting rather than deflating; they all know how bad this performance was. So instead of the easy recriminations, I tried to act naturally, ate a steak and had a drink in the team-room and only indulged in a private inquest over a nightcap with A.C. when the other lads had dispersed.

SATURDAY 4 FEBRUARY As is my custom after a taxing day in the field, I was awake very early. It was not much after 5 a.m. when I tottered to the curtains and stared out into the darkness. Rain was falling and I wasn't certain whether I should feel pleased.

I listened to a tape from Juliet before going down to breakfast. The lads are coming down in different sequence now as we have altered the rooming arrangements since the arrival of Mrs Cook, Mrs Lamb and David Gower's girlfriend. Bob Taylor is now sharing with Tavaré, Marks with Fowler, Cowans with Smith (one to please the anti-apartheid boys), Gatting with Dilley and Foster with Randall. 'Beefy', having temporarily lost his room-mate Lamb, is on his own, and 'Lester' and Mrs Pigott-elect are hopping between rooms because the hotel is so full – a rather unromantic substitute for a honeymoon, I fear.

I have often finished my breakfast before the late-risers have started theirs but today there seemed no undue hurry, for it was still raining when everyone had eaten. I went back to my room, read my book for the first time in a few days, and wondered whether this change in conditions really might prevent a result.

We went to the ground at ten o'clock and there was plainly no imminent prospect of play. The usual rainy-day routine began. Out came the dominoes, the cards, the earphones and the books.

Some touring teams have devoted letter-writers (Geoff Boycott for one) but there was not much sign of scribbling in the dressing-room today. I returned to *The Prodigal Daughter*, interrupting my reading to look at the highlights of a four-year-old New Zealand v West Indies match being shown on television – the torrid occasion during which Colin Croft got himself involved in a barging match with umpire Fred Goodall.

After lunch we watched some televised racing from Ellerslie, near Auckland, and as one selection after another failed to show I was glad I was not wagering money. It is difficult on such days to remain alert and prepared but by teatime I was disappointed by the obvious lethargy creeping into some of our blokes. The rain had ceased and the call into action was threatened, yet some seemed more interested in the sandwiches than the cricket. Considering yesterday's débâcle, I found that strange.

The restart was eventually set for 4.30 p.m. and our nightmare rapidly resumed. Tavaré edged a wide ball from Hadlee, scarcely moving his feet at all, Gower padded up in bizarre fashion to a perfectly straight ball and Randall, going in ahead of Gatting, who has a sore shoulder, was caught at slip second ball, his feet – like Tav's – rooted to the spot.

The procession continued. The dressing-room, haunted, stunned and silent, watched as 'Beefy' was unluckily caught at long leg off a full-blooded pick-up shot against Cairns. Allan Lamb, having played at air a number of times, nicked Chatfield to the wicket-keeper and Bob Taylor was caught at slip.

In ninety minutes play we had contrived to lose six wickets for 44. We stood, or rather quaked, at 53 for seven and to all intents and purposes we were down and out.

All I said at the close was that we would discuss the day in the team-room at seven o'clock. I left instantly, soaked in the bath and listened to Van Morrison while I prepared myself for the speech I must inevitably give to shattered troops.

I delivered the message. I said our performances on the field since the First Test had been unprofessional and largely undisciplined. I said nobody has the right to an automatic Test place, nobody should think they can get by without bothering in the minor games or in the nets. And I said yesterday's bowling was the worst I had ever seen at Test level.

Of today's batting, I pointed out that the sight of a few deliveries

misbehaving (a deliberate understatement) was no reason for international batsmen to play like blind men. We should have been
getting stuck in, giving the crisis blood and guts. But we were
spineless.

I am not a great one for handing out such verbal blasts but I feel
what I said and the way I said it was rational and fitted the bill.
Quite simply, we have looked sub-standard. New Zealand's batsmen manage to forget about balls rearing at their throat – it seems
ours are demoralized by it. And as for our bowling – New Zealand
should have made a maximum of 150. They made more than twice
that figure and there can be no excuses for such philanthropy. It
looks certain to have cost us the match, perhaps even the series.

Amid the general gloomy acceptance of my words there was a
laugh or two . . . A.C. owned up to being stopped for speeding on
the way back from the ground. He was our second such casualty
inside twenty-four hours, David Gower having been pulled over
for jumping a red light last night. It really hasn't been our game so
far.

The evening brightened my spirits a little. Some of us had been
invited out to dinner by John Heslop, a New Zealand friend, and
we arrived at his selfcatering apartment to find his daughters doing
the cooking. It was a splendid meal and I managed to confuse Neil
Foster by telling him not to burn his mouth on the soup. It was cold
soup, a delicacy which, it appears, has not yet reached Fozzy's
remote corner of Essex!

SUNDAY 5 FEBRUARY We began the day needing 55 to avoid the
follow-on. Once we had failed, I knew in my heart it was game, set
and match to the Kiwis. It is over now, completed within three
days and in only twelve hours of actual playing time – the shortest
Test I have taken part in, and certainly one of the worst results.
I am told it is the first time this century England have twice been
dismissed for under 100 but I still point the finger at our bowling
rather than our batting when it comes to assessing blame for the
defeat.

The greatest factor of all was the pitch. No one will sway me
from that opinion. It was just not good enough, and I am convinced
the game should never have been played here. All the necessary
warnings were evident, both statistical – two Shell series games over
in two days – and visible, just by glancing at the square. Yet the New

Zealand officials insisted all would be well and blindly declined to switch the venue. Well, they won the Test, and deserved to. But this was not a true test of playing ability and, at the risk of being labelled a bad loser, I do feel it worth pointing out that the three occasions on which New Zealand have beaten us in the past six years have coincided with three of the worst pitches on which I have played Test cricket – Wellington in 1977–78, Leeds last summer and now Christchurch.

Our lads were not in bad heart this morning, but our fate was soon pretty well sealed. 'Lester' was lbw to Cairns, I survived for a while before losing my middle stump to Chatfield and 'Flash' followed to leave poor 'Gatt' stranded.

After the disasters of the first two days it was no surprise to be following on. I told the lads to forget the first innings and start afresh, and hope I sounded more convincing than I felt beneath the brave front. Tavaré and Fowler gave us some hope, surviving until lunch, but by teatime the match was decided beyond the slightest doubt.

Hadlee, who has had a wonderful match, began the rot with the wickets of Tavaré, normally our most resolute sticker, and Gower, normally our most gifted strokemaker. Neither are at their best at present.

Fowler then fell to Boock's somewhat ordinary left-arm spin for the second time in the match. He never looked comfortable against him and, looking ahead to Pakistan, this does not bode well for his chances against the likes of Abdul Qadir.

Gatting and Botham were out in successive balls to indifferent shots but by now, as so often happens to a team in dire trouble, every shot seemed to be going to hand, every catch was being taken. There was no escape, and a ridiculous run-out just after tea rather summed the whole thing up. 'Flash' went down with all guns blazing, determined to enjoy a final fling, but our total of 93 gave New Zealand an overwhelming win by an innings and 132 runs.

Even before the end of the game I was negotiating for some decent practice facilities here tomorrow, if only so that we may get the seamers bowling basic line-and-length again. The batting may have lacked heart but it was not the main cause of the humiliation – that came on the first day.

Such a defeat is inevitably disheartening but I don't think the mental attitude of our players is too bad. Neither can I bring myself

... v. ENGLAND (2ⁿᵈ TEST) at LANCASTER PARK, CHRISTCHURCH on 3,4,5,X,X FEBRUARY, 1984. TOSS: NEW ZEALAND

IN	OUT	MINS	No.	BATSMAN	HOW OUT	BOWLER	RUNS	WKT	TOTAL	6s	4s	BALLS	NOTES ON DISMISSAL
11.00	12.11	71	1	J.G.WRIGHT	c TAYLOR	COWANS	25	2	42	.	4	52	Edged away-seamer. Pushed forward.
11.00	11.50	50	2	B.A.EDGAR	c RANDALL	PIGOTT	1	1	30	.	.	31	Turned lifting in-swinger chest-high to leg gully.
11.52	12.30	38	3	G.P.HOWARTH*	BOWLED	COWANS	9	3	53	.	2	20	Played square on and inside line – off stump.
12.13	1.00	47	4	M.D.CROWE	c TAVARÉ	BOTHAM	19	4	87	.	2	32	Followed lifting away-seamer. Edged to 1st slip.
12.32	2.39	87	5	J.J.CROWE	LBW	COWANS	47	5	137	.	7	73	Played back and across line of ball that kept low.
1.40	4.03	125	6	J.V.CONEY	c BOTHAM	PIGOTT	41	6	203	.	4	79	Edged outswinging half-volley to 2nd slip.
2.42	4.51	111	7	R.J.HADLEE	c TAYLOR	WILLIS	99	7	281	.	18	81	2nd lb score 99 for NZ (JEFF BECK) Top-edged lifting ball.
4.05	(5.27)	82	8	I.D.S.SMITH †	NOT OUT		32			.	4	48	HIS in TESTS for 3rd successive innings.
4.53	4.59	6	9	B.L.CAIRNS	c TAYLOR	WILLIS	2	8	291	.	.	5	Followed lifting ball – caught in front of 1st slip.
5.02	5.19	17	10	S.L.BOOCK	c TAYLOR	WILLIS	5	9	301	.	.	17	'waaked' – offside edge – simple catch.
5.21	5.27	6	11	E.J.CHATFIELD	LBW	WILLIS	0	10	307	.	.	2	Played back and inside line – 'plumb'.
				EXTRAS	b 8 lb 11	w 2 nb 6	27			0⁶	41⁴	440 balls (inc. 7 no balls)	

TOTAL (72.1 OVERS, 329 MINUTES) **307** all out at 5.27pm on 1st day

* CAPTAIN   † WICKET-KEEPER

BOWLER	O	M	R	W	NB/W	HRS	OVERS	RUNS
WILLIS	22.1	5	51	4	7/.	1	13	32
BOTHAM	17	1	88	1	-/½	2	12⁴	55
PIGOTT	17	7	75	2	.	3	13	50
COWANS	14	2	52	3	.	4	14²	66
GATTING	2	0	14	0	.	5	13	88
		27						
	72.1	15	307	10				

	RUNS	MINS	OVERS	LAST 50 (in mins)
	50	89	18.2	89
	100	130	28	41
	150	203	43.1	73
	200	241	52.4	38
	250	272	59.3	31
	300	320	70.2	48

LUNCH: 87-4 [25.4 OVERS [120 MIN.]] J.CROWE 18* (28 min)

TEA: 203-5 [53 OVERS [242 MIN] CONEY 41* (02) HADLEE 4² (60)]

WKT	PARTNERSHIP		RUNS	MINS
1st	Wright	Edgar	30	50
2nd	Wright	Howarth	12	19
3rd	Howarth	M.Crowe	11	17
4th	M.Crowe	J.Crowe	34	28
5th	J.Crowe	Coney	50	59
6th	Coney	Hadlee	66	63
7th	Hadlee	Smith	78	46
8th	Smith	Cairns	10	6
9th	Smith	Boock	10	17
10th	Smith	Chatfield	6	6
			307	

13 OVERS 1 BALLS/HOUR
4.25 RUNS/OVER
70 RUNS/100 BALLS

© BILL FRINDALL 1984

ENGLAND 1ST INNINGS

IN REPLY TO NEW ZEALAND'S 307 ALL OUT

IN	OUT	MINS	No.	BATSMAN	HOW OUT	BOWLER	RUNS	WKT	TOTAL	6s	4s	BALLS	NOTES ON DISMISSAL
5.39	5.59	20	1	G. FOWLER	BOWLED	BOOCK	4	1	7	.	.	19	Played inside 'arm' ball - clipped off stump.
5.39	4.41	31	2	C.J. TAVARÉ	ct J.J. CROWE	HADLEE	3	2	9	.	.	35	Edged firm-footed push at outswinger low to 1st slip.
4.30	4.48	18	3	D.I. GOWER	LBW	HADLEE	2	3	10	.	.	12	Padded up to late inswinger.
4.42	5.39	57	4	A.J. LAMB	ct SMITH	CHATFIELD	11	6	41	.	2	49	Edged forward defensive push to keeper.
4.50	4.51	1	5	D.W. RANDALL	ct CONEY	HADLEE	0	4	10	.	.	2	Edged outswinger to 2nd slip - pushed forward.
4.52	5.33	41	6	I.T. BOTHAM	ct CHATFIELD	CAIRNS	18	5	41	.	1	31	Picked up short ball - low catch at wide fine leg.
5.35	(12.14)	101	7	M.W. GATTING	NOT OUT		19			.	1	83	
5.41	5.50	9	8	R.W. TAYLOR†	ct J.J. CROWE	CAIRNS	2	7	47	.	.	11	Edged forward defensive push to 1st slip - not at pitch.
5.52	11.14	24	9	A.C.S. PIGOTT	LBW	CAIRNS	4	8	58	.	.	22	'Plumb' - misjudged line and length of slower ball.
11.16	11.54	38	10	R.G.D. WILLIS*	BOWLED	CHATFIELD	6	9	72	.	.	34	Middle stump - played inside and across line.
11.56	12.14	18	11	N.G. COWANS	ct CONEY	CHATFIELD	4	10	82	.	1	9	Edged low to 2nd slip's right - diving catch.
				EXTRAS	b - lb 5	w - nb 4	9			. 6 5 4			307 balls (including 5 no balls)
				TOTAL	(50.2 OVERS, 186 MINUTES)	b - lb 5 w - nb 4	82		ALL OUT at 12.14 pm 3rd day				

* CAPTAIN † WICKET-KEEPER

16 OVERS 1 BALLS/HOUR
1.63 RUNS/OVER
27 RUNS/100 BALLS

BOWLER	O	M	R	W	nb	w	HRS	OVERS	RUNS
HADLEE	17	9	16	3	-	1	1	18	28
CAIRNS	19	5	35	3	5	2	2	16	30
BOOCK	6	3	12	1	-	3	3	15	20
CHATFIELD	8.2	3	10	3	.	.			
			9						
	50.2	20	82	10					

BOWLER	RUNS	MINS	OVERS	LAST 50 (in mins)
	50	103	28	103

WKT	PARTNERSHIP		RUNS	MINS
1st	Fowler	Tavaré	7	20
2nd	Tavaré	Gower	2	11
3rd	Gower	Lamb	1	6
4th	Lamb	Randall	0	1
5th	Lamb	Botham	31	41
6th	Lamb	Gatting	0	4
7th	Gatting	Taylor	6	9
8th	Gatting	Pigott	11	24
9th	Gatting	Willis	14	38
10th	Gatting	Cowans	10	18
			82	

STUMPS: 7-1 [7.1 OVERS 20 MINUTES] TAVARÉ 2*

2ND DAY: RAIN DELAYED START UNTIL 4.30 pm

STUMPS: 53-7 [31 OVERS GATTING 4* (27')] 112 MIN PIGOTT 3* (10')

ENGLAND FOLLOWED ON FOR THE FIRST TIME IN 59 TESTS AGAINST NEW ZEALAND - 225 RUNS BEHIND

© BILL FRINDALL 1984

IN	OUT	MINS	No.	BATSMAN	HOW OUT	BOWLER	RUNS	WKT	TOTAL	6s	4s	BALLS	NOTES ON DISMISSAL
12.26	2.20	75	1	G.FOWLER	c HOWARTH	BOOCK	10	3	25	.	1	62	Edged via pad to silly point.
12.26	1.50	45	2	C.J.TAVARÉ	c SMITH	HADLEE	6	1	15	.	.	36	Edged front-foot push at ball leaving him.
1.51	2.07	16	3	D.I.GOWER	c CAIRNS	HADLEE	8	2	23	.	1	13	Edged (wrist-rolled) stab at offside ball to 4th slip.
2.09	2.45	36	4	A.J.LAMB	c CONEY	CHATFIELD	9	6	33	.	1	26	Magnificent low falling catch (2nd slip) off forward push.
2.22	2.30	8	5	M.W.GATTING	c HADLEE	BOOCK	0	4	31	.	.	8	Edged drive to 1st slip. Leg-break turned.
2.31	2.32	1	6	I.T.BOTHAM	c M.D.CROWE	BOOCK	0	5	31	.	.	1	1st ball - brilliant short square leg catch.
2.34	4.13	79	7	D.W.RANDALL	c CAIRNS	HADLEE	25	8	76	.	2	53	Top-edged cut - held by 3rd slip at 2nd attempt.
2.47	4.09	62	8	R.W.TAYLOR†	Run out (EDGAR/SMITH)		15	7	72	.	2	80	Attempted single to cover - sent back by Randall.
4.11	(4.31)	20	9	A.C.S.PIGOTT	NOT OUT		8	.	.	.	1	14	-
4.15	4.20	5	10	R.G.D.WILLIS*	c HOWARTH	HADLEE	0	9	80	.	.	5	Edged forward thrust to 2nd gully.
4.21	4.31	10	11	N.G.COWANS	c SMITH	HADLEE	7	10	93	1	-	12	Edged vast slog.
				EXTRAS	b - lb 2 w - nb 3		5			0b	9		310 balls (including 4 no balls)

TOTAL 93 (51 overs, 186 MINUTES)   ALL OUT at 4.31 pm on 3rd day.

* CAPTAIN   † WICKET-KEEPER

16 OVERS 3 BALLS/HOUR
1.82 RUNS/OVER
30 RUNS/100 BALLS

BOWLER	O	M	R	W	nb	HRS	OVERS	RUNS	RUNS	MINS	OVERS	LAST 50 (in mins)
HADLEE	18	6	28	5	1	1	17	22	50	131	35.2	131
CHATFIELD	11	1	14	1	2	2	15	21				
CAIRNS	9	3	21	0		3	17	42				
BOOCK	13	3	25	3	1							
		5		1								
	51	13	93	10								

LUNCH: 13-0				
TEA:	65-6	11 OVERS / 35 MIN	FOWLER 8' / TAVARÉ 5'	
		43 OVERS / 155 MIN	RANDALL 16'(6) / TAYLOR 13'(53)	

NEW ZEALAND WON BY AN INNINGS AND 132 RUNS IN 11 HOURS 41 MINUTES OF PLAYING TIME. [MAN OF MATCH: R.J.HADLEE]

NEW ZEALAND'S 3RD WIN IN 59 TESTS v. ENGLAND AND THE FIRST BY AN INNINGS.

THE 15TH INSTANCE IN 976 TESTS OF A SIDE BEING DISMISSED FOR UNDER 100 IN BOTH INNINGS AND 3RD BY ENGLAND (1888 and 1894-95)

WKT	PARTNERSHIP		RUNS	MINS
1st	Fowler	Tavaré	15	45
2nd	Fowler	Gower	8	16
3rd	Fowler	Lamb	2	11
4th	Lamb	Gatting	6	8
5th	Lamb	Botham	0	1
6th	Lamb	Randall	2	11
7th	Randall	Taylor	39	62
8th	Randall	Pigott	4	2
9th	Pigott	Willis	4	5
10th	Pigott	Cowans	13	10

93

© BILL FRINDALL 1984

to accept that we are an inferior side to New Zealand. Last winter in Australia I was depressed at being outclassed and particularly outbowled. I don't believe this Kiwi side are as good as us and I am still full of optimism that we can turn the tide in the Third and final Test.

One lasting impression of the tour to date is the difficulty English players find in adjusting to this type of disjointed itinerary. At home, we are used to playing matches virtually every day of the season; here, the routine is constant nets and frequent international cricket, but precious little in between.

I expressed this view to 'Beefy' over a nightcap and, being an unenthusiastic netter himself, he was fully in agreement. Together, we watched one of the worst films I have ever seen . . . something about a werewolf, starring Oliver Reed. It was so pathetic that it at least made us laugh. Tonight, that was quite something.

5

STALEMATE

MONDAY 6 FEBRUARY Chris Tavaré asked if he could have a chat with me. I wondered whether he wanted to discuss his own grim run with the bat but it wasn't that at all. Instead, he had come up with some very constructive ideas for the team as a whole. He felt it would be a good idea if I spoke individually to the lads to boost sagging confidence. He also suggested we should try to vary the practice routines rather more, to keep people's interest. This should not, of course, be strictly necessary but I know some of our players do get a mental block about nets when they are not in good nick. When we reach Auckland, I think the best scheme will be a competitive open-wicket practice, so that the batters see more point in playing straight and the bowlers can operate under something like match conditions.

I'm glad 'Tav' came to me. He had apparently spoken at length to his room-mate Vic Marks, another who thinks pretty deeply about the game, and I welcome any of the lads making useful suggestions. In some ways, 'Tav' and I are mentally similar. We agreed we are both much more relaxed here than we were last winter, yet neither of us have performed at our best on the field. Tav suggested we may both need to be screwed up to an unpleasant degree to bring out our best – not a likeable characteristic but quite probably an accurate assessment.

During breakfast today, the manager and I decided to release Tony Pigott. Bernard estimates there is a sixty percent chance of Foster being fit for Friday's Third Test and that Dilley is ninety percent certain to be alright. With that encouraging knowledge, we told 'Lester' he could go back to Wellington and rearrange his wedding!

We practised this afternoon. There were no moans, though I sensed it was an unfamiliar discipline to many in the party. At home, where the programme involves almost constant cricket, few players spend much time in the nets once the season is underway.

But on a tour such as this there is no other way of trying to get players back into form and confidence, and I was certainly pleased by the level of effort everyone put in today.

I spent most of the session working on a new run-up. During the Test here, I struggled for rhythm off my full run and obviously sacrificed pace for control when I changed to my short Sunday run. It seemed a compromise was the best solution and, with the help of 'Giff' and his tape measure, I settled on an approach of around twenty-five metres. It felt comfortable and I will definitely persevere with it.

TUESDAY 7 FEBRUARY I was bored enough tonight to turn on the TV in my room and stare vacantly at a couple of six-year-old repeats from the UK. They were so good I can't even remember what they were called. It was that sort of day – every tour has a few, when you travel from place to place and then fill in the remaining hours, living in a kind of vacuum.

Our bags were packed and ready for transportation by 10.30. The flight to Auckland was a painless ninety-minute affair and, when we arrived once again at the Sheraton Hotel, a plush, high-living place, I found 'Beefy' was in the next room to me for the second successive stop. We had a late lunch together, then watched a film called *The Professionals*, starring Burt Reynolds.

There was no practice today but I called the lads together this evening and tried to ensure they were in the right frame of mind for a determined attempt to level this series. Some good points about attitude and motivation came out of the discussion; some, obviously, say more than others but this is thankfully not a tour on which all the talking is done by the elite few.

The social committee then took the stage, applying more hilarious fines for real and imagined misdemeanours – most of them quite unprintable. Banal it may be, but it is more than just a tradition of touring. It lightens the pressure on players, especially if they are feeling down. The humour is instant and would lose almost everything for repetition, but very often such sessions can be hysterically funny at the time.

WEDNESDAY 8 FEBRUARY Today's post was interesting. I opened an air-mail package addressed to me and found some sour grapes in it . . . real ones. The sender introduced himself as a war veteran who had spent much of his life fighting so that the likes of me could play cricket and wanted to know why we moaned in defeat – noble sentiments, but quite irrelevant. I also received a couple of poisonous telexes, including one saying that even Yorkshire, in their current disarray, could play better than us. I shall treat that with the disdain it deserves.

Bernard's reassurances on the fitness of Dilley have misfired. He was still feeling his thigh pretty badly at practice today and we have already discounted him from our Test deliberations. Foster, at least, came through half-a-dozen overs well and, although we did once more discuss calling for a replacement, we have decided to stick with those we've got, even if it means we have to play two spinners in the Test.

The Auckland Cricket Association have clearly made great efforts to get the practice facilities in good order and, as 'Giff' had organized three Worcester players who are coaching here to make up the numbers, we were able to stage a pretty authentic full-scale practice match. The bowling was generally better than the batting. Lamb and Gatting are still not moving their feet very freely and with the exception of Gower, none of the recognized batsmen scored more than 20.

I continued to concentrate on my new, streamlined run, and although I am having familiar trouble with my front foot getting very close to the no-ball line, my rhythm and body-action is much improved. 'Skid' mischievously suggests I am doing it 'to take me into the nineties'.

Tonight I attended the New Zealand Cricket Council dinner at Ellerslie racecourse. Of the four speakers, Alex Dibbs, the new MCC president, was much the wittiest. He has been something of a revelation to us on this tour, showing much greater affinity with our generation than most recent incumbents of his position. He is the sort of man who would march angrily into the hotel kitchens if his breakfast toast had not arrived within ten minutes, but none the worse for that. We have spent several amusing evenings with him already and tonight he was far from disappointing, repeatedly referring to a bet he had struck with Allan Lamb on how long he would speak.

THURSDAY 9 FEBRUARY My routine fell apart this morning when I arrived at the breakfast-room to find a forty-yard queue for tables, mostly made up of Japanese and American tourists. Unlike the average Englishman, who seems to relish queues, I just won't stand in them. So for the first time on a tour, if my memory serves me right, I ordered breakfast in my room.

I spent most of the morning's practice session in the middle of the Number Two ground, giving 'Tav' a personal 'net' and 'Fozzy' a final workout on his injured foot. Of the two, Neil came through better, despite having to put extra padding in his boot to ease the discomfort. Poor old 'Tav' just couldn't get his feet going in the right direction, even after a solid hour of batting. When we gathered to pick the team at lunchtime it was felt that we simply couldn't justify choosing him again, for all the qualities he has so often shown in the past look to have temporarily deserted him.

We discussed the merits of Lamb and Gatting – both are in wretched form but gained a reprieve – and came down against two spinners, chiefly through the memory of Geoff Miller and Phil Edmonds toiling vainly on this ground six years ago. We named a squad of twelve and, depending on the pitch in the morning, either Gatting or Cowans will drop out.

I sought out 'Tav' to break the news privately. As expected, he neither threw a tantrum nor sulked. Instead, he told me he understood perfectly and even wanted to thank me for my loyalty in the past. I was quite touched by the reaction.

Giving the twelve to the press was, on this occasion, as far as I was prepared to go. Keeping back our innermost thoughts and plans has certain advantages and I told the journalists it was up to them to draw their own conclusions about the final eleven. Some of them plainly thought I was being uncooperative but I am not inclined to doing their job for them. One writer asked me the same question in about five different ways before I lost patience and told him he should bring along his typewriter next time so that I could write his story while he waited.

I wandered down to the hotel bookshop and bought *Not a Penny More, Not a Penny Less* to complete my reading of Jeffrey Archer's published works. Personally, I found *The Prodigal Daughter* a disappointment after *Kane and Abel* – but I did get through it.

'Pride' was the keyword of my team talk this evening. I asked for total commitment, all day and every day – even if it seems we can no longer win. Our morale and our reputation took a heavy knock in Christchurch and this is an early chance to restore them. We spoke at great length about the New Zealand individuals, especially about the batting of Hadlee, who must average about 50 against us in recent Tests. I have no doubt at all that we know what to do. The question is whether we can put the theory into practice.

FRIDAY 10 FEBRUARY It would have been living in a fool's paradise to hope for a sporting wicket, so I didn't. We needed the toss, the weather and a shade of luck to go in our favour if we were to have a real chance of winning. But today all three factors conspired against us and all we gained from a good, professional effort was a great deal of frustration.

I had collected my thoughts over another room-service breakfast and I knew what to expect when I went out to study the pitch. Sure enough, it looked very 'flat' and showed no outward signs of giving the bowlers any help at all. We swiftly agreed that five specialist bowlers were essential to the task of taking twenty wickets so Gatting was left out.

When I passed on this information to Geoff Howarth before he tossed the coin he said, 'Surprise, surprise.' When he told me their side would be unchanged, I replied with the same remark. I then wrongly called 'tails' for the third time in the series and knew without being told that we would be in the field.

Bowling off my shortened run, I chose to attack Bruce Edgar round the wicket. It worked. He was out leg-before in my second over, but I was finding great difficulty getting my line right with a strong wind swirling across the pitch. Nevertheless, Ian bowled much better than in Christchurch and Norman Cowans probably as well as he has ever done for England.

It was 'Flash' who had Howarth caught at third slip by Randall. He took the catch at ankle height, which aptly illustrated the pace of the pitch.

That controversially close position which 'Beefy' takes up at second slip was then firmly defended when he clung on to a marvellous catch to dismiss Martin Crowe off my bowling. The ball would have fallen well short of any normally placed slip.

At 111 for three I considered things were going pretty well, and they would have been considerably better if Jeff Crowe had been given out to what looked to me, the bowler, a very good appeal for a bat-pad catch. He was reprieved, which may well be costly.

The weather turned nasty after tea. In fact to be honest I thought the end of the world had come. There was an eerie sort of darkness, quite impossible for cricket. When the light improved sufficiently to resume and we all marched on, it began to rain almost instantly and that was the end of that.

New Zealand are 140 for three with John Wright looking ominously good on 71. He is a fine opener, probably one of the best New Zealand have ever had, but this is the first time in the series he has discovered his touch. For us, it has come at the worst possible time and, with the weather so unobliging, I fear we have not made sufficient progress.

There was little for a captain to complain about in our efforts, however. Foster, not having played since I put him out of action in the nets, was clearly 'in need of the race' and blew hard after only a couple of overs. But 'Skid', whom we have preferred to Cook as our one spinner, bowled only four or five bad balls in his nine overs and there was a great improvement in the seamers who played at Christchurch.

Having said only a couple of days ago that I have felt more relaxed on this trip, I'm afraid I fretted badly today. It even brought on the sort of headache I was often getting in Australia last winter. No doubt it is all down to worry – when the team is under pressure, as we are now and as we were when two-nil down last year, I tend to heap their worries on to my own.

Doug Insole, our manager in Australia, would often tell me there was nothing further I could do. But still I fretted. Eventually, at Melbourne over Christmas, it made me ill. I hope and believe I have learned by the mistake of that reaction, and although today I felt weighed down by the knowledge that we may soon be widely berated for losing yet another series abroad, I think I can shake myself out of it.

SATURDAY 11 FEBRUARY If yesterday was frustrating, today was even worse. I was woken before six by the rain hammering remorselessly against my bedroom window. I looked out on a depressing scene; the streetlamps were highlighting the puddles and the cascading water. It was obvious even at that early hour that we were in for another interrupted day. As things turned out, we were also in for a largely unprofitable one.

We left the hotel at 9.30, more in hope than confidence. It was still raining steadily and a delay was inevitable. Play began only seventy minutes late, however, and in the short pre-lunch session I felt we bowled well. I could not say the same about our performance thereafter.

Wright went on to score 130, most impressively. He is a tidy, conscientous opener but when the opportunity arises he can play shots all around the wicket. I thought I had him plumb lbw, given not out, but three balls later I bowled precisely the same delivery and it bowled him. Enough said.

'Beefy' was in the wars again. Sticking out a boot to stop a straight drive off his own bowling, he took the impact on the foot and hopped around painfully before retiring for rest and treatment, not doing our chances of a breakthrough much good.

Neil Foster was still feeling the effects of his fortnight's inactivity but Norman Cowans again bowled with encouraging life. Given a free rein, he sometimes strays too short to be truly effective, so I had a quiet word urging him to pitch it up another half-yard. Soon afterwards, he got through Coney's defences for a very valuable wicket.

For once, Hadlee did not delay us long, falling to Marks without getting into the groove, but Jeff Crowe gave me ample cause to rue that bat-pad decision going his way yesterday. By the close tonight he had reached 115, never looking such a classically good player as his brother but never giving us another sniff of his wicket. It was a highly competent innings, underlining once again just how far New Zealand have progressed towards a team which has strength in depth rather than relying on a couple of stars.

Ian Smith was with Crowe until stumps and, although he is by no means a weak number eight, the ease with which he was not only surviving but scoring showed up the pitch for what it is. The bowling wore a tired, deflated look in the last session and New Zealand, on 354 for six, have virtually ensured that our chance of levelling the series is dead.

My words to A.C. in Wellington came flooding back. 'If we don't nail them now,' I had said, 'we will really be struggling to win this series.' It looks as if I was right, but I can take no pleasure in that. Tonight, I feel pretty depressed, not to mention weary after the best part of two days' fielding.

I ate some smoked snapper and mussels, which Hedley Howarth had sent to the dressing-room, then returned to lie in the bath and console myself with Bob Dylan's latest album. Confining myself to a glass of water in the team-room, I then spent the evening with Hedley and his wife Louise. They are great hosts, not just for the food they cook and the drink they provide, but because they were sensitive enough not to mention cricket all night . . . and I certainly didn't prompt them.

SUNDAY 12 FEBRUARY Awoke before five. Tossed and turned in the darkness for a while then, despairing of sleep, played one of Arthur Jackson's hypnosis tapes to help me relax. A note in my Injured Jockeys diary informs me that this is the half-way day of the tour. I would like to think it might mark a change in our fortunes.

I ate breakfast with our scorer, Geoffrey Saulez. Geoff has been a fixture on recent tours and his comfortable bulk encouraged the lads to nickname him 'Humphrey' after the fabled bear. I have to report he is not living up to the name, having been on a strict diet since we arrived in New Zealand.

My post brought a welcome letter from Doug Insole, a good friend as well as a good administrator. Apart from offering congratulations, both on my Test bowling record and my daughter, he offered some tongue-in-cheek advice about keeping his Essex protégé Neil Foster out of the nets so that bullying fast bowlers would not hit him on the toe.

Rain was falling yet again at nine o'clock but although the outfield was soggy in various places when we arrived, the umpires decreed that play should start on time. I decided to open with a mixed attack of our quickest bowler, 'Flash', and our slowest, 'Skid'. It was reasonably effective, Cowans in particular troubling the batsmen but having no luck at all when he beat the bat.

Umpire Woodward's interpretation of the lbw law was plainly not in agreement with bowler Cowans's. The batsmen kept playing across the line, missing, and surviving. Frustration would be an understatement.

The New Zealand tail wagged cheerfully in support of Smith, who played within his limitations, applied himself to occupying the middle and showed what can be done on a pitch with no bounce. The batsman can play forward with confidence and if the bowler is foolish enough to drop the ball short it can be dispatched for four without great difficulty or risk.

Considering the circumstances I felt we bowled steadily, if uninspiringly. Cowans was again the pick of the bunch and it is good to see him making such progress and fulfilling his promise of eighteen months ago. Ian, I am afraid, was struggling with his bad foot – just the latest in a series of niggling injuries which have hampered his bowling – and Neil Foster was in danger of becoming depressed over the fact that his Test wickets were costing 70 runs apiece. He has consistently bowled well without getting people out, which is bound to deflate a young and ambitious bowler. He was cheered by the wicket of Cairns, which brought his average plummeting down to 60, and Boock then kneed the ball off middle stump and was inevitably adjudged leg-before.

Chatfield hung around while Smith completed a worthy hundred, celebrating by twice hoisting Marks into the stands for six. His was not an innings which will live long in the memory – the day was too flat and disjointed for that. In all, there were seven short interruptions for showers and poor light, totalling eighty minutes lost. To those can be added another, lighter moment of relief when virtually the entire New Zealand team set off in pursuit of a dog which had strayed on to the ground.

When the last of the weather interruptions brought an early tea, Geoff Howarth declared. They had made 496 for nine, not only clinching the series beyond dispute but leaving us with the job of summoning the motivation to stave off another defeat.

I sat in the dressing-room and thought back over their innings, wondering if there was anything I should have done differently. Probably, I decided, I should have bowled 'Flash' earlier and for a longer spell, though whether it would have made any marked difference to events is questionable. I could think of nothing else. Sure, the rub of the green was not on our side when we most needed it, but the Kiwis played well. I am always trying to instil in our guys the discipline to occupy the crease for long periods; this, I hope, was a lesson to them.

With seven sessions left, our aim was clear. We had to score 297 to avoid the follow-on and save the game. No other option was open. But we could not have made a worse start, for Graeme Fowler fell to the very first ball of the innings, Hadlee slanting it across him and finding the edge. If this distressed all of us, it sent 'Foxy' into a deep depression for a while. He sat in his corner of the dressing-room, slapped on the headphones of his pocket stereo and switched off to the world.

Messrs Cowans, Botham and Taylor were all sleeping off the

effects of our marathon in the field and I sat in the dressing-room watching the closing overs on television. All went smoothly for us until Gower stepped away to aim a reckless forcing shot at the left-arm spin of Boock and was bowled. David's face said it all; he knew he had thrown away a wicket, and it was something we could well have done without.

A couple of appeals against failing light were rejected, but our two South African 'imports', 'Lego' and 'Kippy', saw us through to the close at 50-odd for two, still a mountain to climb if we are to get out of trouble.

With the rest day oasis tomorrow, I indulged in escapism tonight. The Crowe brothers had thrown a party for us at their house and I was delighted to find they had laid on not only copious supplies of food and drink but a lot of vintage Bob Dylan music. I parked myself next to the speaker and sang along, with accompaniment by G. Howarth.

MONDAY 13 FEBRUARY I am a great believer in Test match rest days. Maybe my years are catching up with me but I certainly don't agree with the modern, commercially orientated theory that Tests should be played straight through without a break. Five days is a long time under strain and, even if my mental constitution puts me under greater pressure than most, I feel all players benefit from the opportunity to refresh mind and body for a day. I also don't think it does the spectators any harm, giving them a chance to reflect on what has gone before and anticipate the climax.

On tour, the captain's only regular rest-day duty is to host a press conference, usually around breakfast-time. Today's was a virtual non-event. I gave predictable answers to predictable questions. After all, what can a captain say when his team is faced with simply batting out the match to avert an even heavier series defeat – it's hard to sound inspiring.

I was asked if I thought we had the discipline necessary to bat for two more days. I replied that I can appreciate it is sometimes hard for batsmen to motivate themselves for a lengthy stalling operation but that most of our blokes are in such bad form this would seem the ideal opportunity for them to restore some confidence.

Having failed to eat between Dylan songs last night, I downed some eggs and hash browns – my first cooked breakfast for some weeks – before joining about half the playing strength of the party on a trip to Corbans, a winery owned by the Test sponsors here, Rothmans. On the way we bought some wedding cards to dispatch to Elton John, who gets married in Sydney tomorrow. He came to support us in Australia last winter and we are due to run into him again during the one-day series later this month when his concert tour coincides with some of our matches.

Corbans had laid on the perfect rest-day relaxation. A marquee had been erected on their lawns, next to the vines, and I sat in the shade sampling an excellent choice of reds, whites and vintage port before devouring a portion of one of the three lambs they spit-roasted for us. We all ate well, none better than Mike Gatting who has become known as 'Jabba' after a character in *Return of the Jedi* which eats everything it comes across!

We returned to the hotel late in the afternoon and I spent the evening in my room watching two in-house movies on television – *Hanover Street* and *Stripes* – plus some coverage of the Winter Olympics from Sarajevo. Such quiet, lonely evenings are not to be recommended on a regular basis while on tour. From a distance it might appear to the man in the street that we should all be adopting the Boycott habits of staying in our room, drinking tea, writing letters and going to bed early. But not everyone is made like Geoffrey Boycott. For most of us, such confinement would inevitably lead to morose thoughts of home and the people we are all missing. Soon, homesickness would set in on a serious level and our cricket would suffer. I find it better to remain reasonably active but I had no regrets about changing the routine and spending a few hours alone tonight.

TUESDAY 14 FEBRUARY The nets were unreliable again this morning, which was annoying for batsmen and bowlers alike. The batters lose more confidence than they gain if the ball is flying off at uneven heights and the bowlers feel unable to let themselves go if all they are achieving is the undermining of their own team-mates. So today the batters all had a brief knock on the outfield and I concentrated on bowling to Botham, who still tends to play across the line early in his innings, and to Cowans, who tends to play across the line at any stage.

Cricketers, as I have often related before, are notoriously superstitious. One of the most common superstitions is the belief that, if things are going well in the middle, nobody in the dressing-room should move from what they are doing. So this morning, 'Beefy' decided that we should all take up the positions we occupied while Lamb and Smith saw out the final session on Sunday evening. It may be ridiculous, but no one argued, and I found myself closetted in the dressing-room until lunchtime, reading my latest Jeffrey Archer and trying to keep 'Beefy' occupied so that he would not get bored and resort to some of his favourite practical jokes. He sat and played cards with Marks and Gatting and the superstition worked in that we did not lose a wicket in the two-hour session.

At lunchtime I reassured 'Kippy' that he was playing exactly the right way. He came off very concerned about his slow rate of scoring and, in other circumstances, I would have shared his anxiety. But I told him that our priority was simply to bat out the game and he should not even worry about quick runs. I'm afraid it may not be inspiring to watch, but it is the job at hand.

Lamb was out soon after lunch and returned in high dudgeon over the decision. Stephen Boock had been bowling over the wicket at him to pitch in the rough just outside leg stump. 'Lego', quite legitimately, had been thrusting out his left pad and kicking the ball away, perfectly safe from the lbw law. But when Lance Cairns came on with the new ball he stretched forward to a ball which hit him on the knee and found he was on his way, despite the half-hearted nature of the appeal. After some of the vain shouting we had put in, and especially poor old 'Flash', it seemed an astounding decision – almost as if umpire Fred Goodall had become so bored by 'Lego' padding up that he wanted a change of scenery.

Derek Randall saw us through to tea, by which time 'Kippy' was within sight of a maiden Test century. Sadly for him, he lost the strike for a long period when on 90 and, perhaps feeling nerves more than he might have, he then edged a good ball from Cairns to wicket-keeper Smith and departed for 91. He was extremely disappointed and I felt sorry for him after more than a full day of grafting when his defensive qualities had shone through at an ideal time for us.

Only twenty-five minutes of the day remained when Smith was out and I chose to hold back Botham, particularly in view of the fact that he had been prowling for the past twenty minutes, showing familiar signs of an active bloke bored. I did not want his wicket sacrificed while we were still 60 short of the follow-on mark so I sent in Bob Taylor who, typically professional, kept 'Arkle' company through the closing overs.

Randall was due some congratulations. He has got a problem with the arch of his foot which gives him a lot of pain when he spends any time at the crease, but he battled through it well today. For one whose place never seems secure, at least in the minds of most of the public, he has been one of the outstanding successes of this tour. I don't suppose his character will ever change – he is as comically naive, nervy and uncoordinated now as when I first met him on an England tour in 1976. But his unconventional batting has a habit of being mighty effective and this is by no means the first time on this tour we have had reason to be thankful for it.

It was an altogether better day for us and to lose from this position would require an absolute calamity tomorrow morning. The tempo was slow but occupation was the prime, even sole objective so I never worried about that. Confined to the dressing-room I even got through two hundred pages of my book.

Three tapes had arrived from Juliet when I got back to the hotel and I listened to the first during my ritual bath, which I take whether I have been on the field or not. I then attended the end-of-tour dinner for the Gullivers Travel party with which I'm associated. I had to make a speech, which I never relish too much, but they are a happy and convivial group and no bother at all to me. I left after the speeches and, having had precious little exercise today, walked the mile back to the hotel.

WEDNESDAY 15 FEBRUARY We saved the game, which was all we could hope for. But the series is of course lost and, whether we deserve the tag or not, we have the dubious distinction of being the first England team to be beaten by New Zealand. It is not one of the epitaphs I had hoped for and, as I told the assembled press tonight, I don't like losing.

The facts are these – New Zealand took their one chance of a win at Christchurch, we muffed ours at Wellington. In a three-match series, that is the difference. No one had a chance to win here, on a pitch simply not conducive to any sort of positive cricket.

We had no real difficulty in putting the game beyond New Zealand but the day did have its upset. A.C. called me into the dressing-room during practice and I found he and 'Giff' irate that some of the lads had been messing around in a fielding session while I was elsewhere. I entirely shared their anger. At this stage of the tour, no one has any cause for complacency and before play re-

NEW ZEALAND 1ST INNINGS v. ENGLAND (3RD TEST) at EDEN PARK, AUCKLAND on 10,11,12,14,15 FEBRUARY 1984.   TOSS: NEW ZEALAND

IN	OUT	MINS	No.	BATSMAN	HOW OUT	BOWLER	RUNS	WKT	TOTAL	6's	4's	BALLS	NOTES ON DISMISSAL
11:00	3:13	386	1	J.G. WRIGHT	BOWLED	WILLIS	130	4	265	·	24	297	First first-class 50 of season (3rd TEST). Through gate. HS: Eng 42 (3rd T. F.C.)
11:00	11:08	8	2	B.A. EDGAR	LBW	WILLIS	0	1	3	·	·	2	Misjudged line of ball. angled in from round the wicket.
11:10	1:42	114	3	G.P. HOWARTH*	C' RANDALL	COWANS	35	2	74	·	4	89	Edged drive low to 3rd slip. HS of series
1:44	2:44	60	4	M.D. CROWE	C' BOTHAM	WILLIS	16	3	111	·	3	43	Edged off-side push low to diving 2nd slip's left.
2:46	11:52	382	5	J.J. CROWE	BOWLED	MARKS	128	7	385	·	20	285	(5th in TESTS. (7th F.C. Missed back-foot force - off stump
3:15	4:28	48	6	J.V. CONEY	BOWLED	COWANS	9	5	293	·	·	38	Off stump - played across time.
4:30	4:40	10	7	R.J. HADLEE	BOWLED	MARKS	3	6	302	·	·	7	Played back - bowled off stump by quicker, full-length ball.
4:42	(3:20)	239	8	I.D.S. SMITH†	NOT OUT		113		451	2	9	182	HS in TESTS (4th successive time.) (4th in F.C.
1:54	2:15	73	9	B.L. CAIRNS	C' COWANS	FOSTER	28	8	451	·	4	51	Running catch taken low at wide long leg.
2:17	2:34	17	10	S.L. BOOCK	LBW	MARKS	2	9	461	·	·	17	Played no stroke to 'arm' ball. 21st single figure innings.
2:51	3:20	23	11	E.J. CHATFIELD	NOT OUT		6			·	1	13	Began innings when SMITH was 85 n.o.
				EXTRAS	b - lb 19	w - nb 7	26			2⁶	65⁴	1024 balls (inc 8 no balls)	

TOTAL (off 169.2 OVERS in 688 MINUTES) **496-9 DECLARED**

* CAPTAIN   † WICKET-KEEPER

BOWLER	O	M	R	W	nb
WILLIS	34	7	109	3	6
BOTHAM	29	10	70	0	-
COWANS	36	11	98	2	-
FOSTER	30	8	78	1	
MARKS	40.2	9	115	3	9
			26		
	140.2	45	496	9	

2nd NEW BALL taken at 2:30pm 2nd DAY after 85 overs
- NEW ZEALAND 221-3 after 85 overs

HRS	OVERS	RUNS		RUNS	MINS	OVERS	LAST 50 (in mins)
1	15	31		50	86	20	86
2	14	38		100	165	41.4	79
3	16	42		150	259	64.1	94
4	14	29		200	332	81.4	73
5	16	31		250	372	91.3	40
6	14	67		300	447	109	75
7	13	49		350	513	125	66
8	14	29		400	592	146.1	79
9	17	46		450	644	159.3	52
10	15	54					
11	15	44					

HIGHEST TOTAL AGAINST

LUNCH: 70-1

TEA: 140-3 [30 OVERS]
NO PLAY LAST SESSION - ABANDONED at 6:35pm - 130' LOST

LUNCH: 171-3 [60 OVERS / 242 MINUTES]   WRIGHT 71*(242) / J.CROWE 10'(54)
2nd DAY: START DELAYED 70 MINUTES (12:10 pm)

TEA: 272-4 (CAKEN AT 3:30 - 5 LOST) [73 OVERS / 293 MINUTES]   WRIGHT 86*(298) / J.CROWE 20 (105)

STUMPS: 354-6 [97.3 OVERS / 398 MINUTES]   J.CROWE 72*(210) / CONEY 1*(10)

LUNCH: 416-7 (39 MIN LOST) [130 OVERS / 528 MINUTES]   J.CROWE 115*(346) / SMITH 24*(18)

[151 OVERS / 60 MINUTES]   SMITH 55*(160) / CAIRNS 16*(38)

RECORD 4TH WKT PARTNERSHIP FOR NZ v ENGLAND

---

14 OVERS 4 BALLS/HOUR
2.93 RUNS/OVER
48 RUNS/100 BALLS

WKT	PARTNERSHIP		RUNS	MINS
1st	Wright	Edgar	3	8
2nd	Wright	Howarth	71	114
3rd	Wright	M.Crowe	37	60
4th	Wright	J.Crowe	154	198
5th	J.Crowe	Coney	28	48
6th	J.Crowe	Hadlee	9	10
7th	J.Crowe	Smith	83	120
8th	Smith	Cairns	66	73
9th	Smith	Boock	10	17
10th	Smith	Chatfield	35*	23
			496	

© BILL FRINDALL 1984

ENGLAND 1st INNINGS

IN REPLY TO NEW ZEALAND'S 496-9 DECLARED

IN	OUT	MINS	No.	BATSMAN	HOW OUT	BOWLER	RUNS	WKT	TOTAL	6s	4s	BALLS	NOTES ON DISMISSAL
3.41	3.42	1	1	G.FOWLER	c' SMITH	HADLEE	0	1	0	·	·	·	First ball of innings - edged push at outswinger.
3.41	5.35	457	2	C.L.SMITH	c' SMITH	CAIRNS	91	4	234	·	10	396	Edged outswinger. HS in TESTS (previously 43).
3.44	5.25	92	3	D.I.GOWER	BOWLED	BOOCK	26	2	48	·	2	81	Missed backfoot force into the covers.
5.27	2.38	204	4	A.J.LAMB	LBW	CAIRNS	49	3	143	·	6	190	Beaten by inswing - pushed well forward. 59 min on 49.
2.42	2.30	343	5	D.W.RANDALL	c' WRIGHT	CHATFIELD	104	6	371	·	12	338	(7th in TESTS (25th f.c. Mistimed cover-slash.
5.37	12.25	103	6	R.W.TAYLOR†	s' SMITH	BOOCK	23	5	284	·	4	80	Missed onside slog at leg-break. Smith's 1st Test stumping.
12.27	3.17	130	7	I.T.BOTHAM	RUN OUT [CONEY→SMITH]		70	8	391	2	10	108	Brilliant stop by cover - run refused by non-striker Foster.
2.32	2.54	22	8	V.J.MARKS	c' SMITH	CHATFIELD	6	7	387	·	1	18	Chased wide offside ball. Edged to 'keeper's right.
2.56	(4.56)	100	9	N.A.FOSTER	NOT OUT		18	·	·	1	2	80	HS in TESTS.
3.18	3.31	13	10	R.G.D.WILLIS*	c' SMITH	HADLEE	3	9	396	·	·	11	Edged forward defensive push. SMITH's 5th dismissal (= NZ RECORD)
3.33	4.56	63	11	N.G.COWANS	c' CAIRNS	BOOCK	21	10	439	·	4	70	-
				EXTRAS	b 7 lb 13 w - nb 8		28			3b	51	1373 balls (inc. 8 no balls)	

TOTAL (off 227.3 overs, 773 min) 439 ALL OUT at 4.56pm on 5th day.

*CAPTAIN †WICKET-KEEPER

17 OVERS 4 BALLS/HOUR
1.93 RUNS/OVER
32 RUNS/100 BALLS

BOWLER	O	M	R	W	nb
HADLEE	43	12	91	2	
CAIRNS	40	19	52	2	7
BOOCK	61.3	28	103	3	·
CHATFIELD	46	23	72	2	
M.D.CROWE	17	5	62	0	
CONEY	13	8	13	0	
HOWARTH	7	1	18	0	28→439
	227.3	96	439	10	

2ND NEW BALL taken at 2.35pm 4th day, ENGLAND 139-2 after 88.1 overs
3RD NEW BALL taken at 2.22pm 5th day, ENGLAND 355-5 after 190.1 overs

hb	HRS	OVERS	RUNS
1	1	17	26
2	2	16	26
·	3	18	26
	4	19	44
	5	19	21
	6	16	36
	7	21	39
	8	16	20
	9	17	32
	10	19	22
	11	16	86
	12	16	24

RUNS	MINS	OVERS	LAST 50 (in mins)
50	105	28.3	105
100	208	58.4	103
150	313	91.2	105
200	391	114.5	78
250	499	147.5	108
300	606	179.5	107
350	636	189.0	30
400	717	209.2	81

R.T.P 3.47 to 3.56 (9 min lost) / BLSP 5.45 to 5.52 (7 min lost)

STUMPS: 54-2	[34 OVERS / 122 MIN]	SMITH 16' [22'], LAMB 4' [25']
LUNCH: 123-2	[71 OVERS / 243 MIN]	SMITH 34' [24'], LAMB 45' [146']
TEA: 179-3	[106 OVERS / 363 MIN]	SMITH 71' [363'], RANDALL 19' [98']
STUMPS: 238-4	[141 OVERS / 477 MIN]	RANDALL 54' [72'], TAYLOR 0' [18']
LUNCH: 291-5	[177 OVERS / 598 MIN]	RANDALL 79'(76'), BOTHAM 4' (34')
TEA: 414-9	[219 OVERS / 748 MIN]	FOSTER 8'(66'), COWANS 8' (31')

57 RUNS BEHIND ON FIRST INNINGS
I.D.S. SMITH (5 DISMISSALS) EQUALLED NZ RECORD

WKT	PARTNERSHIP		RUNS	MINS
1st	Fowler	Smith	0	1
2nd	Smith	Gower	48	92
3rd	Smith	Lamb	95	204
4th	Smith	Randall	91	153
5th	Randall	Taylor	50	103
6th	Randall	Botham	87	73
7th	Botham	Marks	16	22
8th	Botham	Foster	4	21
9th	Foster	Willis	5	13
10th	Foster	Cowans	43	63
			439	

© BILL FRINDALL 1984

NEW ZEALAND 2ND INNINGS

57 RUNS AHEAD ON FIRST INNINGS

IN	OUT	MINS	No.	BATSMAN	HOW OUT	BOWLER	RUNS	WKT TOTAL	6s	4s	BALLS	NOTES ON DISMISSAL
5.09	(5.32)	23	1	J.G. WRIGHT	NOT OUT		11		·	2	25	
5.09	(5.32)	23	2	B.A. EDGAR	NOT OUT		0		·	·	9	
			3	G.P. HOWARTH *	⎫							
			4	M.D. CROWE	⎪							
			5	J.J. CROWE	⎬ DID NOT BAT							
			6	J.V. CONEY	⎪							
			7	R.J. HADLEE	⎭							
			8	I.D.S. SMITH †								
			9	B.L. CAIRNS								
			10	S.L. BOOCK								
			11	E.J. CHATFIELD								
				EXTRAS	b - lb 1 w - nb 4		5		0⁶	2⁴	34 balls (inc. 4 no balls)	
				TOTAL	(OFF 5 OVERS IN 23 MINUTES)		16-0					

* CAPTAIN † WICKET-KEEPER

BOWLER	O	M	R	W	Nb	HRS	OVERS	RUNS	RUNS	MINS	OVERS	LAST 50 (in mins)
WILLIS	3	1	7	0	4							
COWANS	2	1	4	0	-							
					5							
	5	2	16	0								

MATCH DRAWN

NEW ZEALAND WON THEIR FIRST SERIES AGAINST ENGLAND (1-0)

MAN OF THE MATCH: I.D.S. SMITH
(Adjudicator: B. SUTCLIFFE)

TOTAL TIME LOST: 4 HOURS 37 MIN.

								RUNS	MINS
13 OVERS	0 BALLS/HOUR								
	3·2 RUNS/OVER								
	47 RUNS/100 BALLS								

WKT	PARTNERSHIP		RUNS	MINS
1st	Wright	Edgar	16*	23

© BILL FRINDALL 1984

88

sumed I told the guys how disappointed I was that their boredom threshold appeared to be so low. Abusing practice like that is a sign of boredom, which is simply a hazard to be borne on any tour. Some of this side don't seem able to cope with it.

Bob Taylor was first out today. That was predictable, but the manner of his dismissal was not – he danced down the pitch to try and hit Boock over the top and found himself stumped by a distance. Botham and Randall, however, were soon putting together another in their series of good stands and, after 'Arkle' departed, spooning a mistimed shot into the covers, 'Beefy' hammered the new ball, chancing his arm while the field was up, then playing sensibly when Howarth put men back. He was on 70, and looking bound for another Test hundred, when Neil Foster almost criminally ran him out. It was a real pantomime dismissal and, wherever the blame lay for the initial muddle, 'Fozzy' was certainly at fault in not trying to sacrifice himself and preserve Ian's wicket.

I am afraid I feel I was a victim of umpiring inconsistency – but I have no reason to complain I should not have been out. Indeed, I am pretty certain I was very much in front when Hadlee hit me on the pad and had his appeal for leg-before rejected, but I was amazed when the next ball brushed my pad on its way to the wicket-keeper and I was given out caught behind. This sort of thing is not uncommon in New Zealand. I will defend their umpires to the hilt against anyone who says they lean towards the home side but I would question the ability of some to give correct decisions consistently.

We survived until shortly before five o'clock because of the dead pitch. Even 'Flash', knowing he would not be smelling the leather of the ball whipping past his nose, got right behind the line and played quite capably for a period.

It left us with only twenty-five minutes in the field and, on such occasions, a captain often tosses the ball to one of his non-bowlers just to provide some light entertainment and fill in the time. For the sake of appearances at the end of a lost series, I decided that was not the thing to do, so Norman Cowans and myself took the new ball as usual and saw the game through with some relatively serious bowling.

New Zealand's officials made some self-congratulatory speeches and various awards were presented; then I dealt, as usual, with the press, radio and television interviews before returning to the hotel, feeling just a shade gloomy.

Bob Taylor told me at breakfast this morning that he had been woken at midnight by an interviewer from his local radio station in Derby. Bob was more polite over the ridiculously late intrusion than I would have been, but the call indicates that the flak will soon be flying over our defeat. I trust we have broad enough backs to take it.

I refuse to believe New Zealand are a better side than we are. I refuse to believe we have done ourselves justice here. But I will admit the coincidence of failure overseas is becoming a little strong. I have never tried to kid anyone that we have a powerful team but I know the ability is there to play very much better than we have managed so far.

As for New Zealand, their team deserves its success. I am not sure the same comment applies to their administration. Going from Christchurch to Auckland was travelling from the sublime to the ridiculous. One pitch produced a result in two days; the other would have struggled to produce one in a week. Whilst the problem is virtually world-wide, if interest in Test cricket, as opposed to one-day cricket, is to be maintained here, let alone stimulated, they must make greater efforts to produce decent five-day pitches.

I didn't leave the hotel tonight. I really didn't feel like it. Unlike some of our young players, who seem to shrug off team defeat and personal setbacks with a worrying shortage of concern, I still take it hard.

6

HONOUR RESTORED

THURSDAY 16 FEBRUARY Our baggage disappeared towards the airport at 7 a.m. and we followed an hour later, leaving behind – among others – ex-president Jimmy Carter. We had watched with fascination last night as he arrived at the hotel with a collection of security guards around him, all, no doubt, wearing bullet-proof vests and carrying at least one weapon. It is apparently the fate of every former president to be surrounded like this but, as I idly mentioned to A.C., surely no one accompanies him into his bedroom? Fortunately, no one here felt inclined to pop him off and all was peaceful as we waved goodbye to Auckland for all of a week.

In Christchurch, where bad memories still abound, we were fitted out with our blue kit for the three one-day internationals but the rest of the day was free. I had a chinese lunch before going to Riccarton races. It was a chilly afternoon but it was good to be amongst racing folk again, even if I did back only one winner in seven races.

David Heard, our genial host here in Christchurch, had laid on a social evening for us at his cricket club, Sydenham. I felt it was a good thing that the guys went to meet some of the locals, as not enough of that goes on these days.

FRIDAY 17 FEBRUARY This squad of ours is full of contradictions. Sometimes the guys delight me with their general spirit and their refusal to ruck when things go wrong. Sometimes they infuriate me by being unprofessional at practice, and today I had to have words.

It disturbs me that a net which misbehaves is immediately seized upon as a reason to shake the head, throw in the towel, even act the fool. This morning, 'Beefy' took to batting left-handed and 'Picca' to bowling off-breaks. I told them both there was nothing to be gained by that and a good deal to lose. When the press write about such behaviour, it will be me who takes the rap. I wanted them to be more constructive, even when the facilities are not good.

Both Norman Gifford and I are becoming increasingly concerned about this part of the players' make-up. It seems to make no difference how often or how forcibly we speak to them about their attitude to practice; for English pros, constant nets are an unfamiliar chore. The batsmen are used to four or five innings each week and they cannot seem to use nets even as a poor substitute. It is all very well them complaining about the itinerary of this tour giving them few match opportunities but it has recently been the players who have spoken out strongly in favour of shorter tours. They cannot have it both ways.

When we sat down to choose the team for the opening international tomorrow we first had to make sure we had an emergency bowler in case any of the five front-line bowlers picked up an injury during the game. Looking through our squad, we were well aware that Mike Gatting was the only possible choice. It is one of the inflexible drawbacks of our squad that most of the batsmen cannot bowl at all, and on this occasion Graeme Fowler was the unlucky man to be left out in order to accommodate 'Gatt'.

We discussed whether 'Gatt' should open with Chris Smith, but David Gower was happy to do the job. Chris Tavaré was certainly considered, in the light of his improved net form and his past record in one-day cricket, but we simply couldn't find a place for him.

So our selected eleven was Gower, Smith, Lamb, Randall, Botham, Gatting, Marks, Taylor, Foster, Willis and Cowans. After telling the unfortunate four that our plans were by no means rigid and that they must keep plugging away, I had a general word with the lads about attitudes. I told them that from the top down, I was not satisfied everyone was giving enough thought to cricket and that in the three hours between then and our next gathering at six o'clock I wanted them all to spend some time considering tactics for tomorrow's game.

When six o'clock came, I found myself being reassured by the reaction to my words. It was a very good team meeting indeed, with almost everyone giving some opinions on one-day tactics and our discussions going so deep that we spent a long while deciding which fieldsmen should be in which position for each of our bowlers. Gatting, Lamb, Botham and Tavaré were the most talkative of the group but I was impressed by the overall level of contribution. It certainly put me in better heart before I left for a dinner engagement with Ian at the home of our racing contact here, Bob McArdle.

Bob had been good enough to take Ian, Norman Gifford and me to see one of the top training establishments in the trotting scene this afternoon. Not only that, he had also arranged for us to try our skills driving the 'sulkies'. To my untutored eyes, the horses in trotting races had always seemed pretty slow from the stands, but when I set off, Beefy in the opposition 'sulky', I honestly had no idea what my destiny might be. Beyond being fairly confident that the horses ought to know their way around the track, I had no idea whether I should be steering, whether the horses should slow down at bends or even how to make them stop. Despite all that, it was a very exciting experience, and when Beefy gave up his 'sulky' for Giff to have a try, I went round another couple of times with him.

While we were enjoying this unusual experience, Bob had been videoing the entire episode and tonight, after dinner, he showed us the evidence of our efforts in glorious technicolor.

I had told the hotel where I could be contacted and a phone call came through from Elton John. 'Beefy' and I both had a chat with him and it transpires that he is going to come and watch us play tomorrow and, by way of return, invite us to his concert on Sunday. I've no doubt most of the lads will snap his hand off.

SATURDAY 18 FEBRUARY It really is amazing how much better one feels after winning. We recorded an overdue international win in a most professional and satisfying manner: the application put in by every member of our side was a joy for a captain to behold.

I could tell as soon as we reached the ground that the lads were very worked up about the game. I like to think that yesterday's harsh words did have some effect but I also have no doubt that the vast interest in one-day cricket here, and the sell-out crowd of around 30,000, added an edge to their nerves.

During the customary meeting of the management team in the middle, we had decided we should bat first in the unlikely event that I could win the toss. But that 20-cent piece of Geoff's came down heads again and, to my great surprise, he chose to field.

This seemed to fit in with our plans, but I was soon having second thoughts about them. Gower was out almost immediately and Smith was run out after spending a lot of overs vainly attempting to find his touch and get the ball away. We were a long way behind the clock when Lamb and Randall came together but they went some way towards pulling us round. Then Hadlee was brought back for a second spell and we promptly lost three wickets in seven balls – Lamb holing out at mid-off, Botham caught behind and Gatting bowled first ball.

We were 109 for five and in a mess. I sat staring out from the dressing-room, listening to the dreadful, all-too-familiar silence and wondering who, if anyone, could pull us out of this one. Randall was still there, but would any of the others stay with him?

Vic Marks provided the solution. Calling on his experience of many tight one-day games with Somerset, he batted with great good sense, within his limitations. With 'Arkle' in his usual impish form, infuriating to opponents, we reached respectability. A score of 188 was nothing to brag about but much better than it might have been.

Acting on last night's meeting, we then went into meticulous detail to get everyone placed correctly in the field. As our plans involved hiding camels like myself where their lack of mobility is least likely to be exposed, it meant I was usually standing at wide slip or point. These are not the best positions from which to direct operations and check on the angles at which other fielders are standing, so I leant heavily on the help of Bob Taylor and Mike Gatting, who was well placed at mid-off to correct any stray fielders and has a cricket brain to be relied upon. The plans were not wasted, and the fielding was suitably sharp to support the endeavour which had gone into getting us all in the right place.

I had trouble early on, bowling some no-balls and several times turning my ankle in a bad foothold. But I did dismiss John Wright, and with the aid of two fortuitous run-outs we soon established control and never allowed things to slip.

Ian bowled very straight and Neil Foster was a revelation. For one so young he showed a tremendous awareness of what is necessary in limited-overs cricket. I am sure he has had a fine upbringing at Essex, for which my old mate John Lever is certainly chiefly responsible. Reluctant as I am to cry over spilt milk, I could not help reflecting on the fact that he may have made all the difference to the Christchurch Test débâcle.

The fast bowler's dilemma struck 'Flash'. He fell between two stools, not being quite sure whether to try to bowl flat out or concentrate on line and length. As a result he was slightly wayward, though not disastrously so.

Vic Marks was very nervous at times, especially when Cairns and Hadlee were aiming to hit him out of the ground, but he kept going well and played his part. What impressed me most was that there was no let-up. New Zealand bat very low down the order, as witnessed by the sight of Ian Smith, who made a Test century only a week ago, coming in at number nine. But not until the last pair were together, more than 50 runs short of their target, did any of our blokes show so much as a smile of satisfaction.

Back at the hotel I phoned Arthur Jackson, friend and hypnotherapist, in Sydney. He was pleased to hear me say I have felt more relaxed on this trip and that I have finally come round to the view that, so long as I can look at myself in the mirror each morning and honestly say I have done everything possible to prepare myself and the team, nothing can be gained by fretting over results.

It is, however, very nice to have an evening when no fretting is required.

ENGLAND v NEW ZEALAND
Played at Christchurch, 18 February 1984

England won by 54 runs

ENGLAND 188 for 9 in 50 overs (D. W. Randall 70, A. J. Lamb 43, R. J. Hadlee 5 for 32)

NEW ZEALAND 134 in 42.1 overs

SUNDAY 19 FEBRUARY As we have three clear days before the second of the limited-overs matches, we gave the lads a rest today. As usual, they each used the free time in their own ways. Having lent Ian Botham my car so that he could go fishing, I busied myself at the hotel and made the arrangements for tonight's Elton John concert. In all, they are supplying us with twenty-three tickets, which is more than generous.

I had a drink with some of the press guys then went to Sunday lunch with the Heards. In the middle of a long stay overseas, a plate of roast lamb and roast potatoes can help one feel a little closer to home.

A fleet of cabs transported our party to the concert, where we were met by one of the promoters and taken to the VIP area backstage. Elton and his wife Renata were there to chat to us and I couldn't help but be struck by Elton's relaxed, conversational mood with a performance only a matter of minutes away. I compared his approach to a big night with mine on the morning of a Test and decided that, in this respect at least, we must be complete opposites.

There were 21,000 in the audience, virtually all standing, and although my unusual height enabled me to see the stage without much difficulty, some of the other lads struggled – especially when blokes in front of us lifted their ladies on to their shoulders. It was, however, a memorable night; when Patti Moyston, Elton's press secretary, said we would be welcome at the next concert, which happens to coincide with our stop-over in Wellington, the response was enthusiastic. We had a long, cold wait for taxis but nobody seemed to mind, and even that inconvenience was cut short when the obliging promoter organized cars for us.

MONDAY 20 FEBRUARY There are times when I feel I worry too much about this job, other times when I am convinced others don't worry enough. But tonight I was reassured to hear Geoff Howarth relating his own experiences of the cares of captaincy. We were at a barbecue together when the subject arose. Oddly, although we have long been good friends, we had not discussed it before and I was slightly taken aback when 'Kiwi' told me how he suffered from the pressure so much that, once, he was physically sick in the dressing-room through the strain of it.

This, however, was not the most stressful day of the tour for either of us. The middle of a one-day series never seems to hold the same tension as the middle of a Test. Perhaps my priorities are old-fashioned, but to my way of thinking the two forms of cricket will never remotely compare in importance. Having lost the Test series, though, we are very determined to get things absolutely right in what is left of our stay and I will not be wholly satisfied with anything less than a three–nil win.

We practised on the Wellington ground this afternoon after a thirty-five-minute flight from Christchurch. I asked Ian to organize a fielding game for the rest of the lads while I put in some work with Norman Gifford on my run-up. This got them all loosened up before I joined them for a catching session. 'Giff' took the bat and hit a series of skiers, shouting the name of the player who was to take the catch. This is a well-known routine which we must do sixty or seventy times on tour. The difference today was that a great deal of the catches – more than I have ever seen before, in fact –

were put down because the white ball was so difficult to sight against the clear blue sky. The point of practice is, of course, to iron out such problems and I trust we will locate the leather rather more easily tomorrow. But one of my gripes about one-day cricket in the Antipodes is the insistence on using white balls; I fully appreciate their necessity for night games but, from the players' viewpoint, I can see only drawbakcs when they are used by day.

TUESDAY 21 FEBRUARY An early start. By 7.30 a.m. I was on the way to a local junior school, where I had been asked to chat to the kids before they began lessons for the day. It is a measure of the current New Zealand cricket boom that such interest is being very vividly shown in schools around the country. The boys here were clearly thrilled to see and listen to me and, given the opportunity, it is the sort of thing that could be done much more frequently by players on overseas trips.

Managed to grab a quick breakfast back at the hotel before another practice session at the ground. Most of the catches were held today but then there were clouds in the sky. Perhaps we could use a dull day for tomorrow's game.

My new run-up now measures precisely 73 feet 3 inches. 'Giff' confirmed this with a tape measure today and, as I did not even get my front foot near the no-ball line, I have some margin for error. In the past, such successes at practice have turned out to be no more than a fool's paradise when it matters, but I shall certainly try this new run again tomorrow and hope for the best.

There was little I could tell the press at the customary eve-of-match conference. The selectors had conferred during practice and decided there was no point in meeting formally as the team would, unsurprisingly, be the same as had won in Christchurch. We did call a team meeting for this evening, though, and before getting on to tomorrow's match we gave the lads a few early hints as to what they should and should not do when we reach Pakistan next week. It does no harm to put some thoughts in their heads but obviously we will be discussing the second leg of this trip in much greater detail at the end of the week.

It is not often that we can look back on our previous performance and conclude that we did nearly everything right. But tonight we did, and I am in no doubt that we need only reproduce the all-round professionalism of our Christchurch efforts to win again.

This, however, is virtually certain to be a higher scoring match and so could produce quite different pressures.

Once our meeting had broken up I went straight back to my room for a very quiet evening, listening to tapes and watching the television. I was in bed by ten but before I could drop off to sleep the phone rang. It was my brother ringing from Sydney to tell me that he has decided to see out one last term in his teaching job there before returning to look for work in England. Good news.

WEDNESDAY 22 FEBRUARY Cricket would be a far less complicated game if every side played at their best all the time; in fact, it would probably become boring. But heartening as it was today to take part in another thoroughly capable and convincing victory, it was at the same time exasperating to think back on the sub-standard sessions which cost us the greater prize in the Test series.

After this win we must now decide whether to keep this combination in an effort to score a three-nil whitewash or change the side to try and play one or two of the strugglers into better form. My own instincts tell me that there is nothing like winning to boost the morale of players, so we should remain unchanged, but it is a pleasant dilemma to have after all the earlier headaches.

The public are plainly clamouring for more one-day cricket here. It is not a move of which I would approve and the New Zealand authorities are going to have to find a happy medium to satisfy players and spectators alike. The fact is, the ground was full to capacity by 9.30 this morning and it was as much as the staff could do to clear the outfield of spectators so that we could practise.

At least the toss went to form. I called tails, it fell heads – the same old routine for the fifth successive international game. Geoff chose to bat but our bowlers again rose to the challenge. Franklin and Edgar were soon bogged down and I decided to alter the rehearsed rota and try Vic Marks early. If they were to accelerate and take 'Skid' for the number of runs they undoubtedly hoped, they would have to hit him over the top.

Even I had not reasoned the move might have quite the success it did. Vic soon had Franklin caught-and-bowled, then bowled a frustrated Edgar, dismissed Howarth leg-before and the two Crowe brothers, both caught at mid-off. Dramatically soon in the proceedings, New Zealand were reeling at 63 for five and V. J. Marks came off guarding figures of five for 20.

Many a one-day game has been turned on its head from such an apparently decisive position but, this time, we never really had another moment's worry. Foster and Cowans bowled well against the two dangermen, Coney and Hadlee, and, despite a few stray deliveries from messrs Botham and Willis late on, we picked up the remaining wickets at a steady rate and they were all out for 135. The fielding was excellent, matched by the level of encouragement handed out to each bowler in turn. It was very good to see the lads gritting their teeth with the will to win. There were times earlier on the trip when I wondered what could be done to induce such devotion to the job.

Even the batting went much better than of late. Gower looked more confident until both he and Lamb were out attempting to hit the ball over the top, not an easy task on this pitch. But Randall, for whom failure has become a rare event on this tour, was as solid as ever in support of Chris Smith, who grew rapidly in conviction and, remarkably, scored 60 of his 70 runs in boundaries. The rate required was down to just two an over by the time 'Kippy' departed, his job well done, leaving Botham to try and finish it off in his most outrageous style. He failed, falling to an atrocious reverse sweep with one needed to win – a run eventually secured when Randall upstaged Botham by making contact with a similar though better-constructed shot and dispatched Cairns for four. In the circumstances it did not seem worth chiding either of them for flamboyancy – it had been a marvellous win in every other respect.

At the press conference I perpetuated my reluctant habit by criticizing the wicket. It is not something I do lightly. There was another enormous crowd in the ground today and, like the great majority of one-day cricket followers, they came in hope and expectation of seeing strokes played and runs scored. I could have told them after a very few overs that they were in for a disappointment; on this surface, the bowlers always held the upper hand with batsmen forced to commit themselves to shots which would otherwise have been condemned as reckless in a time-limit game on such a wicket.

Elton John came into the dressing-room for a beer and a chat after the game and, tonight, four of us went to see him in concert again. 'Beefy', 'Skid', 'Foxy' and myself made up the party and, this time, we watched the performance from backstage, standing ten feet away from the band in the wings. It added a new dimension, being able to see the reaction of the audience to each song, and by the end of the night I was croaky from singing along.

ENGLAND v NEW ZEALAND

Played at Wellington, 22 February 1984

England won by 6 wickets

NEW ZEALAND 135 in 47.1 overs (J. V. Coney 44, V. J. Marks 5 for 20)

ENGLAND 139 for 4 in 45.1 overs (C. L. Smith 70)

THURSDAY 23 FEBRUARY Thinking ahead to the inevitable long, boring evenings to come in Pakistan, I went shopping for reading matter. Playing safe, I bought the latest Dick Francis paperback, *Banker*, and, experimenting, I took the recommendation of a lady in the shop and selected a book I had never heard of called *The Ninja*.

With the entire day free, I then set off to walk to the harbour, and along Marine Parade, before catching a cab to a fish restaurant where I had arranged to meet some of the guys for lunch.

The afternoon was spent signing fifty miniature bats and dealing with a pile of correspondence relating to the Pakistan leg, which is beginning to loom a little ominously in the minds of some. Having had some problems there myself, six years ago, I can see no benefit in telling the new boys that it will not be as bad as they have heard if, in reality, it is even worse. Naturally, in a company of this sort, there have been some hideously humorous stories told about the worst of the conditions. It is best, I think, to approach it in light-hearted way while making everyone aware of what discomforts they might be about to encounter. It will then come as a pleasant surprise if things have improved since I was last there.

FRIDAY 24 FEBRUARY We left at 7.30 this morning and I was not sorry to be moving on. Our hotel in Wellington has not been the brightest or most welcoming place I have stayed, and my own room was particularly dark and dismal. It seemed we had arrived in Auckland to nothing better, however, because the supposedly top-class Sheraton Hotel had no rooms prepared for us and we were asked to wait in the lobby for an hour. Instead, we opted to go to the ground in our travelling uniforms and, there, changed into cricket gear for an unscheduled early practice.

Yet again, the nets were poor and the batsmen could hope to achieve nothing more than keep their eye in with the feel of bat on ball. We concentrated on fielding and then, back at the now ready hotel, the selectors convened for a discussion on whether to choose tomorrow's side on current merit – in other words, making no changes – or to reshuffle, giving the enforced idle some action, in the light of the series already being won. I remained much in favour of retaining our winning combination and, hopefully, our momentum, and vice-captain Gower supported this view. Although the case was won, we still have slight doubts about Randall, who has a blister, and Foster, who has a sore ankle, so there may yet be a chance for one of the others.

The danger at this stage is complacency, though God knows we have little enough reason for it. Nevertheless, I tried to drum into the players tonight the need for utter determination to complete this part of the job with another win. I said no one must relax until after the game, when they were free to fill their stomach with the food and wine they would undoubtedly be missing in Pakistan.

I was pleased, again, by the volume of constructive ideas. It was thought that we should aim to repeat the ploy of bringing on 'Skid' early in the New Zealand innings, although this time circumstances may be rather different. Both Franklin and Edgar have been dropped to make way for Webb and Wright, so there is every chance that they will be away to a much quicker start unless they lose wickets.

Elton is in town again. It seems that his tour could have been planned to coincide with ours – but none of us are complaining about that. The four of us who have attended both concerts to date went to dinner with the man and his entourage tonight, and a convivial and animated evening was had by all. Sitting next to Elton, we compared the problems of cricketers with footballers, about whom he is well qualified to talk through his position with Watford, and also compared the pressures of sportsmen and entertainers. I found myself being fascinated by his appetite for work after fifteen years at the top of his profession. Not many cricketers could claim such a record and Ian, for one, freely admits that he would find enthusiasm impossible after such a long run. Elton's thoughts on

I. T. Botham also made interesting listening: having studied him on two overseas tours now, he feels we gave Ian too long a lead in Australia last winter and ought to have kept him more under the thumb. Perhaps he is right.

I was back in the hotel by eleven o'clock and managed to read a full half-page of *The Ninja* before falling asleep. Maybe that lady's recommendation was not so good, after all.

SATURDAY 25 FEBRUARY As soon as our bus came within sight of the ground this morning it was obvious that it takes more than two defeats to turn the New Zealand public away from one-day cricket. There was another huge crowd – and, this time, they were not disappointed.

The pitch looked placid and I thought we should bat first, but held out little hope of doing so. The toss was surely beyond me. Indeed, when Howarth threw up his usual, lucky 20-cent piece, I just called 'the usual' and waited for it to come down 'heads'. But it didn't. I told Geoff I was too shocked to make a decision, but managed to pull myself together enough to tell him he would be in the field.

We began badly. Smith, troubled several times during a fine first over from Hadlee, was neither forward nor back to the last ball and lost his off stump.

Reassurance followed swiftly. Gower and Lamb batted splendidly, first negating the early setback and then accelerating to such a healthy degree that they appeared to have laid the perfect platform for a formidable score. A major innings from Gower was probably more important than anything, so low had his confidence dropped, but it was not to be. Tragically, he was the victim of a dubious lbw decision from umpire Kinsella and returned to the pavilion looking suitably dejected with life.

We lost our way from that moment on. Randall was bowled attempting an unconventional and, frankly, unwise legside hit against Boock. Just as Botham had begun to look threatening, he was well caught by John Wright off a straight hit. Then Gatting was adjudged caught behind – after having to wait for what seemed like half a minute for the decision – and we were down to the odds and ends. It was now a question of using up the overs and giving Lamb as much of the strike as possible. These tactics, although theoretically sound, produced three run-outs and I found myself going out to bat for the final over, something I had not expected. 'Lego' was still there after an encouraging return to something like his best, and between us we squeezed the total up to 209, which was about 30 short of a reasonable target.

The Kiwis, noisily urged on by the enormous crowd, had put in a very fine fielding effort on a bumpy outfield and Ewen Chatfield, who excels in this kind of cricket, was once more the pick of their bowlers.

I feared the worst, silently. Out loud, I told the lads we would win if we could turn in another high-class performance in the field, and took appreciative note of the ebullient confidence they plainly felt after our two recent wins. It did not seem misplaced, either, when I removed Webb and then successfully summoned Marks for another early spell, Wright giving him his wicket with a mistimed drive. 'Skid' continued to bowl well, but the later New Zealand batsmen had learned their lesson against him; he was allowed to complete his stint cheaply but without further success and it was the seamers who were then taken to task as we drifted steadily towards a heavy defeat.

Martin Crowe and Howarth played so soundly that the only way we looked likely to separate them was by a suicide case through some eccentric running. The run-out chances came and went, agonizingly untaken, and it was soon clear that our total was nowhere near enough on such a good pitch. Botham and Foster lacked penetration and, in desperation, I turned to Chris Smith for a few overs of his gentle off-spin. Such dabbling with occasional bowlers has been known to work miracles, but it didn't this time. I brought back 'Beefy' again and he rewarded his ego, if nothing else, by dismissing Howarth lbw. The excellent Crowe and the solid Coney were beyond even a flutter of panic, however, and a dissatisfying day for us ended with listening to a few more speeches heaping praise on today's New Zealand effort before, almost as an afterthought, the Rothman's Cup was presented to us.

Richard Hadlee was named 'man of the series', which embraced both the Tests and limited-over games. He did win the Christchurch Test, and with it the series, almost single-handed, so it was by no means an unexpected decision though some of our lads felt that Derek Randall had contributed more, over a greater number of games. There were no hard feelings though and we were soon swapping our blue gear for the Kiwis' brown in the time-honoured style of footballers after the Cup Final, before sharing a few cans of beer in the dressing-room.

At seven o'clock, we said farewell to the New Zealanders for the last time, wishing them well for their forthcoming trip to Sri Lanka and accepting their good wishes for our journey into Pakistan.

Ian and I then went to our third Elton John concert – just as good as the previous two – before rejoining the rest of the lads for the party Elton was throwing for us in his suite. He certainly gave us a fine send-off. I certainly enjoyed myself. And I am not exactly sure what time it was when I struggled off to bed.

ENGLAND v NEW ZEALAND
Played at Auckland, 25 February 1984

New Zealand won by 7 wickets

ENGLAND 209 for 9 in 50 overs (A. J. Lamb 97 not out, D. I. Gower 35, E. J. Chatfield 3 for 29)

NEW ZEALAND 210 for 3 in 45.3 overs (M. D. Crowe 105 not out, G. P. Howarth 72)

SUNDAY 26 FEBRUARY My head reminded me of last night. Rapidly and painfully. But after two months away, and with virtually a week before our next competitive cricket, a hangover seems no great sin. Just an inconvenience.

I ate some breakfast before taking a call from the Elton John suite. Remarkably fresh, the entourage were now serving buck's fiz. It would have been churlish not to join them . . . so another humorous and convivial few hours got underway, various of the players and management dropping in as we chatted through funny events during our matches and their gigs.

They all call each other by their job rather than their name. So Patti is known as Publicity, Elton as Artiste, Bernie Taupin as Scribbler, and others as Producer, Promoter etc. This emerged as we ate a delicious English-style Sunday lunch to the strains of Elton's uncompleted forthcoming LP.

The kindness of Elton and his crew, especially to Ian and me, have been quite staggering. I think they enjoyed having us around and the feeling was certainly mutual. Too much high living on a tour is obviously to be discouraged but this past twenty-four hours has been a perfect way to end the New Zealand leg and prepare us for the more spartan existence to come.

7

GAME, SET AND MATCH TO ABDUL QADIR

MONDAY 27 FEBRUARY Few people, I was saying at the start of this diary, actually look forward to touring Pakistan. I can't say I feel like an exception to that rule today. A month stretches ahead in which most of us can expect to endure unpleasant conditions, unpleasant illness and probably some less than exhilarating cricket. Imran Khan, we hear, is still injured and will miss the series; it does not take Mensa intelligence to deduce that the Pakistanis are now unlikely to inject any great life into the Test pitches.

My job as captain, however, is clearly to prevent the players moping or moaning. We wanted the shortest possible tour of Pakistan and we have got it, so there can be no valid excuses made about the itinerary. It is up to us to make the most of it and, primarily, to try and salvage something from our second Test series of the winter. God forbid it should be as disappointing to us as the first.

My morning duties today included the statutory winding-up operations. I was in the team-room by nine o'clock with A.C. and the man from the local bank, sorting out the end-of-tour finances, a necessary chore. Then I met some of the other guys in the three rooms we had kept on until our afternoon flight and, along with Ian, went into the town to raid a delicatessen, stocking up for our journey into the unknown of Faisalabad for the Second Test. We bought tinned ham and turkey, smoked oysters, seafood paté, crackers and crispbreads and then, satisfied with the haul, indulged ourselves with a hamburger at Macdonalds. None of us can be sure what food will be available in Pakistan. We hear the hotels in Karachi and Lahore are new and well-equipped, but it is better to be safe than starving.

Enjoyed a luxurious bath and composed a final tape for my wife. I won't be trusting any to the fickle Pakistani post. I also listened to a new tape by Van Morrison I had bought in town. It must be good – even A.C. voiced his approval.

There was something markedly different about our collective

appearance when we left the Sheraton Hotel for the last time, shortly before four. The social committee, gaining in invention, have decreed that we must all be clean-shaven for the entry into Pakistan. They have not yet revealed how long this must continue but the removal of beards and moustaches has left messrs Smith, Botham, Lamb, Tavaré and especially Gatting with a strikingly unfamiliar look.

At the airport we followed the usual patterns of the long-distance flier, buying paperbacks and duty-free, saying a few farewells and then sitting around in that tedious vacuum peculiar to airport departure lounges around the world, nothing left to do but drink coffee, study the idiosyncracies of other, equally bored passengers and hope to hell the plane is not delayed by mechanical failures or mechanical unions.

Well, we took off on time at least, and, quickly changing from our smart tour uniforms into casual travelling clothes, we settled down for the long journey to Bombay, via Adelaide and Perth, on a British Airways Jumbo. The steward was soon running around fetching food and drink, all the lads being keen to stock up in case of shortages in either department on arrival, and the usual in-flight entertainment of cards, music and books were quickly in evidence. All seemed well for three hours. Then the captain came on the loudspeaker.

One of the 747's four engines had been shut down after showing a fault, he reported, and we were now diverting to Sydney.

We sat on the plane for a while after landing and then came the announcement that we should go to the transit lounge while the aircraft underwent various checks. I took the chance to phone my brother, but within an hour we were summoned back on board and took off again. This time, however, there was not even time for the drinks to be served or the cards to be dealt. We were in the air no more than ten minutes before the captain relayed the dismal news that the same fault had reappeared and that he intended to dump most of the aircraft's fuel at sea before returning once more to Sydney. It was late, and the news was not welcome.

Resigned, now, to a night stop-over, we disembarked and set about the long, boring rigmarole of identifying luggage. A.C., hankering after efficiency as ever, pronounced himself unimpressed with the operation. He was possibly still less impressed when, after much confusion, we were directed by rumour, rather than an airline official, to the nearby Hilton, where we found there were insufficient rooms to go round. A.C. had to share.

TUESDAY 28 FEBRUARY Soon after seven o'clock we congregated in the lobby, a bedraggled sight in the travelling clothes which were all we had brought from the airport. Some of the lads had taken the opportunity to visit old friends, or favourite haunts, in Sydney. We all hoped there would be no further diversions to the plan.

British Airways had abandoned the repair job on yesterday's aircraft and provided a new one. By nine o'clock we were once more airborne, installed this time in the 'bubble' cabin upstairs in the Jumbo, a pleasant, private way to travel.

Elton's latest album *Too Low For Zero*, was played and played again on the lads' personal stereos, virtually all the way across Australia. Leaving Perth behind, we were treated to two movies. I watched only half an hour of an uninspired Dudley Moore film and did not even bother to put on the headphones for John Travolta and Olivia Newton-John in *It Takes Two* – not my scene at all.

Time passed, quickly at first. But the final three hours dragged, until the lights of Bombay's bleak and poverty-stricken airport side came as welcome relief to me and as an exciting sight to the craning heads of those new to the sub-continent.

We were mercifully only required to wait twenty minutes on the ground before boarding a PIA 707 and I decided this was the moment to remind the lads of their responsibilities. Before anyone else came on the plane I told them that, tired though they were, I expected them to look the part of international cricketers when we arrived in Pakistan and to be civil to the throng of people who would surround them in the arrivals lounge.

It took less than two hours to reach Karachi. I resisted dinner, having eaten four or five meals on the British Airways flight, and tidied myself up before we landed.

The press and photographers swarmed around A.C. for twenty minutes while I did two television interviews. Then it was my turn to be bombarded with questions from all directions and, like the other lads, garlanded with red flowers.

We were ushered straight through customs, all fears about being searched for hidden alcohol apparently unfounded. Our next worry, however, was not so easily overcome and, weary as I was at eleven o'clock at night on our second day of travel, I had to face it.

A.C. and I sat in a room at the Holiday Inn, our base for the next week or so, being filled in by the British Consul, Peter Streams, on what are evidently very serious threats by students to disrupt the series. We already knew something of their grievances and their avowed intentions as rumours had reached us in New Zealand, prompting A.C. to phone Lord's and request them to seek re-assurances about our safety. Although I have no doubt the threats made headlines in British papers, I certainly never believed there was any danger of the tour being abandoned. Students are power-ful in Pakistan and have been behind a number of the riots affecting Tests in recent years. But once we accept the fact that we are under-taking to tour there, we are by inference accepting all the time-honoured risks. And these include student riots.

Peter Streams certainly seemed confident that everything pos-sible was being done in terms of security around the team and the grounds. He could not predict the students' actions but said we may know more tomorrow.

Having completed that business, we checked that our provisions had arrived from England. They had, which took a great weight off our mind. Supplies of food and water for Faisalabad, and some gin for consumption in the team-room, lifted our spirits, though so far, I must say, things don't seem as bad as they might have been.

WEDNESDAY 29 FEBRUARY My second sleeping tablet of the tour had ensured a full quota of rest but I woke at 7.15 feeling disorientated, not sure what time it was nor, briefly, what country I was in. The scene outside the window of my modern, carpeted and well-equipped room was typical of the sub-continent, the morning mist hanging over the mosques, the dusty streets below and the kite-hawks, enormous and menacing, circling overhead. There were some pleasant gardens across the road from the hotel and, as I had first noticed on the bus from the airport last night, things seemed cleaner than I recalled from my previous visit six years ago.

Normally, after such an arduous journey, I would gladly have declared this a rest day. But with only forty-eight hours before the First Test begins, that was plainly impossible. By 9.30 we were on the way to the National Stadium in two mini-buses with a police outrider. It was a twenty-minute drive and, in daylight, I was able to confirm my impression that things have changed considerably here. New hotels have sprung up, new office-blocks abound and the poverty is nowhere near as striking as it can be in Bombay or Calcutta, for instance. It is, however, extremely bright and hot and the conditions are not those I would ideally choose for cricket.

What seemed an enormous Pakistani squad was already present when we arrived at the ground – they have apparently been in training here since Sunday. Only one net was available to us and, as all eight batsmen needed a knock, it was evident we were to have a longer session than we had originally planned. I told the bowlers to divide the net bowling amongst themselves so that nobody did too much or too little and, considering most of the lads are still understandably dozy and blinking at utterly foreign conditions, I was quite pleased how they all coped.

A.C. had established that food could be brought from the hotel to the ground for our lunches during the game. The alternative to this is either to eat the local provisions – usually spicy and hardly befitting the English sportsman's stomach in the middle of a hot day – or to go without. As the hotel seems singularly well run, we are happy to put our trust in them.

Suitably encouraged, I called a team meeting at six this evening and told the team I considered the country had improved dramatically on all the evidence available so far and that they must not get down in the mouth because things could be very much worse. We went on to a High Commission party, peopled largely by expatriates from England and serving apparently unlimited drinks, then returned to the hotel for an excellent meal in their Chinese restaurant. All things considered, it has been a perfectly acceptable day.

THURSDAY I MARCH We chose our fourth different combination of opening batsmen in four Tests today, desperate measures for any touring side. While it would be wrong to claim any of us are supremely confident about this one providing the elusive success, the pairing of Smith and Gatting was a logical process rather than a wild gamble and was the only selection which occupied the committee for any length of time. We settled on Gatting because he plays the spinners competently and is likely to be facing them pretty quickly. We discarded Fowler, who struggled against Boock in New Zealand and would have to face three spinners here, and Tavaré, who is still being embarrassed in the nets. Cowans won the last bowling place ahead of Foster and Dilley on the strength of his showing in the Auckland Test.

We had made an early start for the ground after a breakfast which, for me, now consists of Weetabix (in warm milk), toast (made with gooey white bread), honey (imported from New Zealand) and coffee (instant). Today, our police escort was rather larger, but there was still no sign of any trouble and we were inside the ground by 8.30 – before, in fact, the groundstaff had even erected the nets.

With two nets instead of one to work in, things were much easier and everyone except yours truly had a bat. Apart from Tav's continued struggles, David Gower showed no great confidence and Derek Randall did not look impressive: but then, in the nets, he never does. Lamb and Botham hit the ball well after making tentative starts and this, at least, was encouraging.

We were told that as security arrangements at the ground were now complete we could leave our kit overnight. There is a police presence here the like of which I have never previously seen on the day before a Test. No chances are being taken. I wish I could say the same about our team selection, but I am afraid the element of risk is inescapable in our efforts to find the right combination. The overriding problem is that, on all my ten previous tours, I have never known so many batsmen out of form at one time.

Before announcing the side to the players, and then the press, I sought out 'Gatt' and told him he would be opening. His feelings might have been mixed; he knows that, in a sense, this could be his last chance to establish himself in what has so far been a sadly disappointing Test career for one so murderously prolific in county cricket. He has yet to make a hundred for England, yet he reels them off with great regularity for Middlesex. It is the old, familiar story. Test bowlers have the ability to expose technical flaws which can remain easily camouflaged at county level. Allan Lamb has encountered similar problems. Watch him play for Northants and he looks a world-beater, but he too has not fulfilled his potential for England. I believe one of his problems is that he plays defensive strokes too rigidly, with the bat a long way in front of the pad and sometimes even held one-handed. Far too often, this leads to him being caught in the short-leg area.

Gatting's failing has often been a tendency to play across the line early in his innings, resulting in too many lbw dismissals. I very much hope he comes through this new challenge successfully, not just because it will aid us in winning this series but also because I have an ever-increasing respect for Mike's cricket brain. He expresses himself fluently and has very sensible ideas about field placement and tactics. A year as Middlesex captain has plainly brought him on a great deal.

His inclusion as opener is not the only risk we have taken. Nick Cook has not bowled in a match for more than a month yet comes in here as a front-line weapon – if this pitch helps any bowler, it will surely help the spinners. 'The Beast', however, possesses a fine touring temperament and, while I am sure he would prefer to have had some recent activity, he will adapt.

We had another team meeting at six o'clock, chiefly tactical but also an opportunity for me to outline the procedure in the event of crowd trouble. I did not wish to alarm anyone unnecessarily, but neither can we afford to have players reacting in a dangerous or provocative manner. If missiles are thrown at players fielding near the boundary they should move undemonstratively into the middle and report it; if there is any sort of riot we must observe the fundamentals of staying calm and staying together.

Pakistan, I then pointed out, are formidable opponents in their own country and if we are to avoid (a) defeat and (b) depression, we must be positive in our attitude. That, however, does not mean being extravagantly aggressive and the spinners must get used to bowling to a run-saving field before they can expect to attack.

The social committee took the stage once the serious business was complete, and I am now happily convinced they make a good team. Before leaving Auckland, they had spent most of the money from the fines and a good deal of effort buying a present for each member of the party, depicting an occasion when each of us made a fool of ourselves. For this leg of the tour, when evening entertainment will be somewhat limited, they have also introduced a 'Wally of the Day' award. Whoever makes the day's major gaffe must spend the evening wearing a costume purchased for the purpose, comprising a sickly brown shirt, garish yellow tie and hideous teapot hat. The first recipient is Graeme Fowler, who happens to be on the social committee!

With jet-lag still a problem, I almost fell asleep during my meal in the coffee-shop, and tottered wearily to bed at 8.30, early even for me on the night before a Test.

FRIDAY 2 MARCH Concerted wailing outside my window woke me before six. It took me a while to locate the source of the racket but it turned out to be the calling of the faithful to morning prayers at the mosque. We are hardly entitled to expect the Pakistanis to alter their religious customs just so that we can get some sleep before a big day, but I could have done without the early call all the same. Listened to Vivaldi's *Four Seasons* before breakfast and felt better for it.

Most of the lads were in the breakfast-room before 7.30. This would normally be cause for astonishment, some of our party being notoriously reluctant risers, but as the arrangement here is that a buffet breakfast downstairs is included in the room rate, A.C. has rightly insisted that everyone should make the effort to come down for it.

An early start was, in any event, compulsory, as we had arranged to leave for the ground at 8.15 to be sure of getting through the traffic in good time. The police escort had grown again, quite dramatically this time, and now included a motor-cycle outrider, armed guards on our bus and twenty more in a truck following behind. They were comforting, though again idle.

Once on the ground, Zaheer, who has replaced Imran as Pakistan's captain, called me over to discuss the match conditions with the umpires. The rule here is a minimum of 77 overs per day, which seems a small number despite the days being half-an-hour shorter than in England. 'Zed' and I were just about to toss when Mudassar Nazar tapped his skipper on the shoulder. They shared a few words in Urdu before 'Zed', by way of translation, told me that Mudassar 'had some problems' and they left the field together. When 'Zed' returned a few minutes later he brought the news that Mudassar was unfit and his place in the side would be taken by Ramiz Raja, younger brother of Wasim Raja.

My usual call of 'tails' was successful for a change and I gleefully picked up the coin and said we would bat.

If we were tense as the game began, there was clearly some tension being felt outside, too. The crowd was small but the police and army were there in their hundreds to guard against trouble. Even in our dressing-room we had constant protectors armed with sub-machine guns or revolvers, and I noticed they were also stationed on the stand above us and at all other vantage points around the ground.

But things remained quiet, off and on the field. Our progress was slow, but that did not concern me at this stage. The important thing was that neither Smith nor Gatting looked in any trouble, even when the two spinners made their predictable early appearance. Lunch was imminent when 'Gatt', playing forward to the off-spin of Tauseef, unluckily caught his bat behind his pad and the ball gently hit the top of the off stump. It was a blow, but our experiment had been a qualified success.

Lunchtime was an unusual experience, in that it lasted ninety minutes instead of forty. This is apparently now the custom on Fridays which are the equivalent of our Sundays, so that the locals are able to leave the ground for prayers. We ate our excellent lunch provided by the hotel's Chinese chef (soup, chicken in batter, chow mein and ice cream) before Norman Gifford and I took the non-players for what must be a virtually unique lunch-interval practice on the outfield.

David Gower had joined 'Kippy' and there were no alarms until just before tea, when Smith played an uncontrolled square drive at Sarfraz and was caught in the gully. This was again an irritating and potentially dangerous time to lose a wicket; no batsman likes going in just before a break, and Lamb only narrowly survived the rest of a particularly fine over by Sarfraz.

The real trouble began after tea. Lamb played that one-handed defensive shot against Sarfraz and it brought his dismissal again and Randall, having played one optimistic sweep for four against Abdul Qadir, followed up with a dreadful, darting drive across the line of a googly and was bowled middle stump. We were now 108 for four and any further loss tonight would have spelled disaster. Somehow, we got through, although Ian could have been out any time early on. He makes little pretence at being able to pick Qadir and although he struck him straight for six, he never looked likely to repeat the shot.

By the close we were 147 for four and defending resolutely. David had played very sensibly and was just past 50, his first Test half-century of the tour. It might have been worse but remained a disappointment to me, having gained first use of a very good pitch. We needed to be aiming for 350 or more and we do not look likely to get it. The most daunting aspect of the day was that Qadir did not bowl at his best, yet still perplexed our batsmen.

I honestly begin to wonder what sort of surface our batters could score runs on. They certainly find some extraordinary ways to get out.

The evening was spent in front of the team-room video. It was a film called *The Fog*. Some of the boys found it frightening and went to bed early; I found it tedious and watched it all, yawning through the last hour. There seemed nothing better to do.

SATURDAY 3 MARCH Pakistan days are long when you wake up at 4 a.m. I tried to read my book, tried to doze, gave up both and got up early for breakfast.

I was optimistic, rather than confident, that we might get ourselves out of trouble and build a respectable total, a hope that was swiftly shattered. We lost Ian in the second over, misreading Qadir and caught at short leg; then 'Skid' fell into Sarfraz's leg trap; two lbw verdicts we did not greatly care for cost us the wickets of Taylor and Gower; and Nick Cook and I were both caught at gully. Some while before lunch we were all out for 182, a very sorry effort.

Mohsin Khan and Qasim Omar, one tall and slim, the other short and stocky, cruised past 50 for Pakistan's first wicket and I feared we would be in the field for a very long time. But when I brought 'Beast' on for the twentieth over, the whole day – and maybe the game – changed course. He was tense for a couple of overs, bowling too flat and too short after his long lay-off. But in his third over the confidence was suddenly there, the loop and flight returned and, immediately, he had Omar in two minds and trapped him leg-before on the back foot.

Ian donned a blue headband and began to bowl with more purpose from the other end. Our cricket had changed character and, with lots of encouragement being passed around, everyone soon began to expect further wickets. They came, too.

Ramiz, the debutant, went forward to Cook and was given out, caught at silly-point. Clearly disgusted with the decision, he stood at the crease for an eternity. I wonder if he was told about it – no player in my side would get away with behaving like that.

When Zaheer came in, 'Beefy' pleaded with me to have a man back for the hook. I agreed, but 'Zed' ducked the bouncer. Ian bowled another one short, this time wider of off stump, and it was cut, hard and head-high, to gully, where Lamb took a fine catch. This was a real bonus. The searing heat and the bright light was making my head ache but I could put up with that. Pakistan had lost three wickets for 13 and we were back in the game.

Nick bowled two loose overs after tea before regaining his

rhythm. Mohsin, who had reached an impressive 50, perished to a hot-headed drive and then Wasim, who found himself reluctantly tied down for half an hour, obligingly hit a long-hop straight down mid-on's throat.

For the last forty minutes I used both spinners, but they did not bowl as well as I would have liked and the day was seen through by Salim Malik and Anil Dalpat, the new Pakistan wicket-keeper. Nonetheless, they had plunged from 67 for nought to 131 for five, which constituted a fine fightback, and I was delighted with the character of our performance on another blazingly hot day. What did amaze me was that there was hardly anyone watching. The students have so far been conspicuous by their absence yet it seems their threats may have kept a lot of peaceful fans away, too. We did hear talk of a demonstration outside the ground tonight and there were still a lot of police around when we left in our bus. But no trouble.

I had a shower, the hotel water not being hot enough for a proper bath, then sat down with the lads to watch *The Dirty Dozen*. We amused ourselves putting names of our tour party to the faces of the convicts when they were introduced at the start of the film. Another fun night at the Karachi Odeon . . .

SUNDAY 4 MARCH It is often easy to look back on a day and pinpoint any number of incidents which significantly altered the direction of the game. Today, one stood out a mile and the great irony is that the 'culprit' was Nick Cook, in all other respects the hero of our effort. Abdul Qadir was on one and Pakistan were six wickets down and still some way behind when Nick dropped a hard, but relatively straight caught-and-bowled chance. Matches are not won by 'if only's' but none of us could help looking back and rueing that moment, because Qadir went on to share a lusty and profitable stand with Salim which took Pakistan into an irritatingly healthy lead.

I had not hesitated to open our attack this morning with Cook and myself. My rhythm and pace was as good as it has been at any stage of this tour but, annoyingly, the no-ball epidemic was back and every time I got things right I was far too near the front line, often over it. I did manage to have Dalpat well caught by Bob Taylor, diving forward, before Qadir was reprieved and the grip we had begun to exert on the match was loosened.

Qadir was eventually out off a short ball from Botham so I brought back Cook against the new batsman. The move worked, Sarfraz quickly being caught at slip when a delivery bounced unusually. With the new ball available straight after lunch I was still full of hope that our deficit would not be too daunting, especially when I ended Salim's fine innings leg-before. But there was yet another twist to come, the unlikely last-wicket pairing of Tauseef and Hafeez, who has three fingers of his right hand missing, frustrating us for a considerable time. When I eventually caught Hafeez at mid-on Pakistan's lead had grown to 95 and there were some long faces on our side.

The pitch was still benign, as I could testify. It had been very hot either side of lunch and, for a quick bowler pounding in on that unyielding surface and trying to extract some life, it was backbreaking if not heartbreaking. That, however, gave us no copper-bottomed guarantees against another batting collapse and I watched rather nervously as we began our second innings half an hour before tea.

My worst fears were realized. Gatting, playing no shot to Sarfraz and thrusting his pad outside the line of off stump, was adjudged lbw. I could see no way in the world that the ball would have hit the stumps, an opinion the television replays supported. But he was out and that was that. Bad went to worse when Smith was authentically leg-before to a very good nip-back delivery by Sarfraz and we found ourselves 21 for two, still 74 behind.

Tired from our efforts in the field, I sat in an easy chair and watched the rest of the play on television, surprised by the quality of the colour and the camerawork and the variety of replays. Gower and Lamb battled it out well and the deficit had been reduced to 40 by the close. With two days left we are going to have to play extremely well to win now, but clearly any result remains a possibility.

Tomorrow is a rest day and, as usual on the evening before, we were chalked down for an official engagement, this time a dinner hosted by the Wills tobacco group, Pakistan's Test sponsors, at the nearby Intercontinental Hotel. We were forewarned that the food would be curry and the drinks nothing stronger than Coke, so I took the necessary steps. The yearning for curry that I frequently have at home has certainly not manifested itself in this country, so I had some room-service food before departing. We also shared out some of our stocks of alcohol to fortify us for a 'dry' evening.

What we had not expected was that, before the dinner began, we had to stand for a recital from the Quran, the bible of the Muslims, read in Urdu. It might have baffled us in English, but in Urdu it was incomprehensible.

MONDAY 5 MARCH The 'wailing' seems to kick off each morning at ten minutes to six. It was loud enough again this morning to deprive me of a rest-day lie-in, so I got up and tried to compose a tape for my wife at home. Frankly, so little happens here off the field that it is hard to find much to say.

The press conference, which on rest days in other parts of the world is sometimes a duty to be discharged before escaping to more pleasurable pursuits, was today the only engagement on the horizon. I told the assembled writers I thought our first innings total was more than 200 short of ideal and, although we had since done quite well in the field, we were now in a very tight corner.

They went away to compose their pieces while I stayed in the team-room to discuss the state of the tour with A.C. We soon got around to the dismal form of the batsmen and agreed that at least part of the fault lay in the lack of any pressure on middle-order players such as Gower and Lamb. There is so little talent available to present a challenge that they have come to be sub-consciously sure of their places; and no one with that complacent cushion is likely to show quite the hunger for runs and success that he would with more competition. The fact remains, however, that it would take a brave band of selectors to leave them out.

I filled in an hour this afternoon with a visit to a suede and leather shop, conducted by our friendly armed guard and a smooth-talking salesman who confessed to having once gone bust in London's Liverpool Street. He still managed to persuade me to part with a good number of rupees, however. Some of the other lads had visited the shop earlier in the day and 'Flash' Cowans won the 'Wally' outfit for trying on a full-length black leather coat, in which the guys claimed he became quite invisible.

David Brown, good friend and Warwickshire manager, phoned tonight and we spent a few amusing minutes chatting about Karachi. The last time he was here, fifteen years ago, the Test ended prematurely with England's players making a hasty retreat from a particularly nasty riot and escaping to a homeward-bound flight under the cover of darkness. I was able to reassure Dave that, while some things here will never change, nothing of that nature had threatened us yet.

One of the things which appears totally unaltered here is the deplorable standard of the telephone system. Juliet managed to get through to me from England three times tonight, in itself a minor miracle, but her first call was cut off after two minutes and her second after ten seconds.

With the evening entertainment once again restricted to an unchanging room-service menu and some uninspired videos, I went to bed, feeling rather low, at 9.30.

TUESDAY 6 MARCH Defeat came a day early and, although it was not by as ignominious a margin as had once seemed likely, it was every bit as depressing. Pakistan, needing to score a mere 65 to win with a day and a half to get them, panicked and lost seven wickets. We might even have had cause to imagine we were unlucky, but such a dramatic finale could not totally disguise the inadequacies of the performance which had put us in the mess.

For the second time in the game we collapsed pitiably with the bat and, although Abdul's beguiling leg-breaks and googlies were predictably the main cause of the shambles, our blokes' desperate form was at times caricatured by their struggles against lesser bowlers. It is certainly not through lack of net practice. By this stage of a tour the majority of batsmen usually find nets superfluous to their needs but, this morning, all the main batters with the exception of Gower had a knock. Gower is a notoriously reluctant netter but one can hardly criticize him for not practising more here as he made the top score in each innings.

My own day went wrong from the start. During fielding practice I misjudged a skier and took a painful blow on the end of the little finger. It is swollen and disfigured now, and Bernard Thomas believes I have probably cracked the bone. He treated it with a cold spray and strapped it, but it was a bad omen for the day.

Qadir, to give him his due, bowled extremely well. Our batsmen face precious little leg-spin in England, and none remotely approaching the quality of this little man. I have no doubt he is a delight to watch when you are not among the opposition but, to us, he is becoming as much a psychological danger as a physical one and this is something I must work on.

His ability to deceive and disguise was swiftly evidenced this morning. Lamb was caught behind, playing inside the leg-break, and Randall was bowled playing horribly outside the googly. It was an identical shot to the identical ball which accounted for him on Friday, so he has clearly learned no lessons. He knew it, though, and returned to the pavilion muttering 'same bloody shot' time and again.

'Beefy', who could still make nothing of Qadir, appeared to decide he must make hay at the other end and was bowled round his legs sweeping at Tauseef. Then Vic Marks, who looks in a worse tangle than anyone against Qadir, lunged desperately at the googly and was bowled. At lunch all our hopes rested with Gower, who was past 50 again and proving the suspicion that Qadir does not enjoy bowling to left-handers (this, he claims, was the reason for his lack of success against Australia, whose top order is crowded with them). But David fell soon after the break to the off-spinner and I think we knew in our hearts we were doomed.

There was a period of sensible play from Cook and Taylor. Their secret was to play Qadir largely as a googly bowler, so covering the ball which turns into the bat. The logic of this is that it doesn't matter then if the leg-break beats you by a foot so long as you have the off stump covered. This show of logical thought was cut short by an unfortunate incident. 'Beast', facing Wasim Raja, was given out, caught at slip, when it was clear even from the boundary that the ball had bounced well in front of Mohsin. But the fielder continued to claim the catch and the umpire's finger was up. Nick should have swallowed his pride and walked off, but instead he stood at the crease gesticulating, probably exchanging words with Mohsin when, after an age, he began to trudge off. I took him aside later and told him that, no matter what the provocation, that sort of behaviour was completely unacceptable. I like to think England have set a high standard of sportsmanship under my captaincy and I don't want him tarnishing that reputation.

Just to rub salt into the wound, Bob Taylor was also controversially adjudged caught off bat and pad, but there was no doubt at all over my capitulation to Wasim, and the scoreboard showed we had mustered a miserable lead of 64.

The crowd, which was bigger than on the first three days, were now noisily beginning their celebrations. But in the next couple of hours we departed from the script to produce a finish which stopped

ENGLAND v PAKISTAN
First Test

Played at National Stadium, Karachi, 2, 3, 4, 6 March 1984
Pakistan won by 3 wickets

England

C. L. Smith c Wasim b Sarfraz	28	– lbw b Sarfraz	5
M. W. Gatting b Tauseef	26	– lbw b Sarfraz	4
D. I. Gower lbw b Qadir	58	– c Mohsin b Tauseef	57
A. J. Lamb c Ramiz b Sarfraz	4	– c Anil b Qadir	20
D. W. Randall b Qadir	8	– b Qadir	16
I. T. Botham c Ramiz b Qadir	22	– b Tauseef	10
V. J. Marks c Ramiz b Sarfraz	5	– b Qadir	1
†R. W. Taylor lbw b Qadir	4	– c Mohsin b Tauseef	19
N. G. B. Cook c Salim b Qadir	9	– c Mohsin b Wasim	5
*R. G. D. Willis c Wasim b Sarfraz	6	– c Tauseef b Wasim	2
N. G. Cowans not out	1	– not out	0
L-b 6, n-b 5	11	B 6, l-b 6, n-b 8	20

1/41 2/90 3/94 4/108   182   1/6 2/21 3/63 4/94   159
5/154 6/159 7/164 8/165 9/180   5/121 6/128 7/128 8/157 9/159

Bowling: First Innings—Hafeez 11–3–21–0; Sarfraz 25.3–8–43–4; Tauseef 24–11–33–1; Waṣim 3–2–1–0; Qadir 31–12–74–5. *Second Innings*—Hafeez 8–3–14–0; Sarfraz 15–1–27–2; Qadir 31–4–59–3; Tauseef 21–6–37–3; Wasim 3.3–1–2–2.

Pakistan

Mohsin Khan c Botham b Cook	54	– b Cook	10
Qasim Omar lbw b Cook	29	– c Botham b Cook	7
Ramiz Raja c Smith b Cook	1	– c Botham b Marks	1
*Zaheer Abbas c Lamb b Botham	0	– b Cook	8
Salim Malik lbw b Willis	74	– run out	11
Wasim Raja c Cowans b Cook	3	– c Cowans b Cook	0
†Anil Dalpat c Taylor b Willis	12	– not out	16
Abdul Qadir c Lamb b Botham	40	– b Cook	7
Sarfraz Nawaz c Botham b Cook	8	– not out	4
Tauseef Ahmed not out	17		
Azeem Hafeez c Willis b Cook	24		
L-b 5, n-b 10	15	B 1, n-b 1	2

1/67 2/79 3/80 4/96   277   1/17 2/18 3/26 4/38   (7 wkts) 66
5/105 6/138 7/213 8/229 9/240   5/38 6/40 7/59

Bowling: *First Innings*—Willis 17–6–33–2; Cowans 12–3–34–0; Botham 30–5–90–2; Cook 30–12–65–6; Marks 13–4–40–0. *Second Innings*—Willis 2–0–13–0; Cowans 2.3–1–10–0; Cook 14–8–18–5; Marks 12–5–23–1.

Man of the Match: Abdul Qadir

Umpires: Khizar Hayat and Shakoor Rana.

just short of the miraculous. It was a fool's paradise to think we could win with so few runs to defend but we did at least expose the suspect Pakistani temperament: under pressure, they flap.

'Flash' bowled only one over with the new ball before I brought on Cook. I bowled two at the other end, then summoned Vic Marks. But it was Cook who had the instant success again, first removing Omar and then his tormentor Mohsin.

Zaheer, to my surprise, was obviously very nervous. He hit a couple of fours off 'Beast' but was bowled trying to hit a third. The crowd sensed an emergency. So, slightly more cautiously, did we. I chivvied everyone up to keep the outcricket tight and hoped to hell that the circumstances would inspire rather than overcome two spinners who are relatively inexperienced in Test cricket.

We were helped immeasurably by a run-out which accounted for Salim; then Ramiz, perhaps remorseful, was caught at slip off 'Skid'. When Wasim came in, I posted a man deep on the long-off boundary and, to my immense gratification, he fell into the trap. 'Flash' held the catch superbly, spinning like a shot-putter to prevent himself toppling over the boundary line, and then rushing towards the middle with those white teeth bared in a euphoric grin. Pakistan were 40 for six. I could hardly credit it.

I made my mistake here, failing to bring back a seamer against Qadir and Dalpat. They played sensibly against the spin and put on 19 runs. Too many. Even when Cook dismissed Qadir, his fifth wicket in the innings and his eleventh in an incredible match performance, the odds were stacked in Pakistan's favour. It heaped irony on the situation that Sarfraz provided the winning runs with an edge through the slips for four. But it was really no more than we were entitled to expect.

After I had been into the Pakistan dressing-room to congratulate Zaheer and his players, we all had to troop across the ground for some presentations underneath the television stand. Qadir was man of the match. Despite Nick Cook's marvellous performance, we could not argue, as Qadir had not only bowled brilliantly but done much to decide the game with the bat.

The interviews took almost an hour and I said the same thing each time. We simply didn't make enough runs and we must learn, fast, how to counter Qadir. I intend that we should start tomorrow. This is the first time an England side has been beaten in Pakistan and I am not keen on it happening again under my captaincy.

8

INJURIES, ILLNESS AND INNUENDOES

WEDNESDAY 7 MARCH The muck-raking has begun. A.C. had a call from Lord's today to check out a story which appeared in this morning's *Daily Express*. It revolves around a broken window in the room occupied by Ian Botham and Allan Lamb when we were in Hamilton, almost two months ago. It is true there was a breakage, but the damage was paid for promptly and everyone appeared to have forgotten about this very minor upset. But I understand the *Express*, not content with dragging up a story more dead than dated, has spiced it up with all kinds of innuendoes. I find it amazing, not to say annoying, that certain sections of the press will go to such lengths to kick a team when they are down. We are by no means the first sporting side overseas to suffer this apparent obsession with putting the blame for defeat on anything, so long as it is more sinister or sensational than simple poor form or limited ability.

What with one thing and another, I am not in the best of moods tonight. We had a worthwhile morning, rigging up a net on the Test wicket and bowling on a rota system to each of the batsmen, but things began to go wrong when we arrived at the airport for our afternoon flight north-east to Lahore. We have to transport so much kit on tour that our baggage always exceeds the weight limit imposed by airlines. Special arrangements are generally made in advance so that we do not have to keep paying excess charges, but the PIA representatives at Karachi airport today denied any knowledge of this and demanded more than £200. A.C. produced all kinds of paperwork during the ensuing argument but it would seem the blame lies with the recent changes of personnel in the hierarchy of the Pakistan Cricket Board, and a subsequent breakdown in communications.

The aircraft was full, the cabin heat was oppressive and the landing was erratic. We must have bounced the first hundred yards and then, when we came to rest an equal distance from the terminal building, we all had to get on a bus, which took a circular route of about 450 yards to the arrivals door – a journey we could have walked in about thirty seconds. The frustrations of travel in the sub-continent.

Just to make matters worse, it transpired that two of our precious cases of gin and whisky had been broken. It was that kind of day.

THURSDAY 8 MARCH For some reason that I have yet to discover, the wailing begins a good bit earlier here. It woke me at 4.30 this morning, which did not bode well for our stay in Lahore. My first impressions of the Hilton are that it does not stand comparison with Karachi's Holiday Inn. When we return from Faisalabad next Saturday, however, it may well seem a palace.

This is where the tour reaches its cluttered climax. We have a one-day international tomorrow followed by two Test matches starting on successive Mondays. We then finish the tour with the second one-day international the following Monday. It is a taxing schedule but not one we can complain about: the idea was to confine our commitments here to as short a timespan as possible.

We practised at the ground this morning. The Gaddafi Stadium is a more impressive and better-tended ground than Karachi's and has a greener, flatter outfield. Being much further north they receive a good deal more rain here; indeed, the entire city has more colour than the somewhat anaemic complexion of Karachi. There were two net wickets prepared, of which the one designated for the Pakistanis looked much the better. But they had not arrived, so we used the 'first come, first served' principle.

With no other competitive cricket available, we decided that the four guys who did not play in the Test should have a game tomorrow. Bob Taylor would stand down, albeit reluctantly, allowing Graeme Fowler to keep wicket. Nick Cook would take a rest, partly because we were not keen for the Pakistanis to have too close a look at him. Norman Cowans's groin strain solved another place and he would rest up for the next Test. And Chris Smith stood down to prevent us having too many openers. Having made these decisions it was a bit depressing to see most of the lads still so badly out of form in the nets – the majority were 'out' four or five times in a fifteen-minute innings on a very reasonable surface.

Our tactical meeting tonight concentrated on the problems posed by the restriction of the match to forty overs a side. Although bowlers are allowed to come off full runs, the game will be more akin to a John Player contest so it will be necessary to take a fairly defensive stance early on. We have a long batting line-up and I called on the batsmen to put on a sharp display of running between the wickets in order to put the Pakistani fielders under pressure. My turn had arrived to be nominated 'Wally of the day'. The evidence produced was a picture of me in a local newspaper advertising the merits of a certain shaving cream. It appeared the day after I had managed to persuade the social committee to scrap their recently-introduced shaving ban because I considered some of the lads were looking scruffy. It was, as they say, a 'fair cop'.

I donned the clown's outfit, which effectively decided that I would be taking my dinner in the team-room. Over tandoori chicken I chatted with 'Beefy' and 'Lego' about the *Daily Express* story and its implications, trying to reassure them that they had no need to worry. Now, however, stories have reached us from various sources that other London newspapers have dispatched news writers – as opposed to sports writers – to dig for scurrilous gossip about us and imply we were beaten in New Zealand due to our off-field behaviour. I have warned all the lads to be very wary and I feel sorry for them. They are trying their guts out; it is not their fault if they are not good enough.

FRIDAY 9 MARCH Tonight we have problems on every conceivable front. We have lost another one-day international, we are apparently about to be accused of drug-taking in New Zealand and we may well be losing Ian Botham injured for the rest of the tour. Seldom can so much have gone wrong for a touring team in a single day, and it is hard to know which to worry about most.

The match came first. I had suffered another near-sleepless night and was wide awake long before the mosque loudspeaker started up at 4.30. I have now discovered, incidentally, that of the five times each day the Muslims must pray, the first must always be before sunrise. The reason that the Lahore alarm call is earlier than Karachi's is due to the angle of the sun, which is all-important to the Muslim faith. Fascinating as such facts may be, they did not stop me feeling weary when I went down to breakfast.

We had problems getting through to the ground, indicating an enormous crowd. Just as in New Zealand, it would seem the Pakistani cricket-lover is neglecting Tests in favour of one-day games – a great shame. With a 9.30 start scheduled we were on the ground at what seemed a fairly uncivilized hour, yet the terraces were already packed when Zaheer called me over for the toss, won it and put us in to bat.

Pakistan had also made a number of changes, in their case the aim being to bring in a few medium-pacers common to the limited-overs game. None of them remotely approach the still absent Imran in class, but they did their job adequately and ours was once more an innings of fits and starts. Fowler and Lamb played well but there was no cohesion in our performance, no partnership of substance. In a forty-over game, one aims to have plenty of wickets in hand for an onslaught in the final six or eight overs; things did not work out that way and our total of 184 was, I considered, about thirty short of what we needed.

A curious clause in the match conditions meant that lunch could not be taken until we had bowled two, fruitless overs. I didn't eat, partly because I seldom do when a hot afternoon in the field awaits me, partly because I had begun to feel my recent lack of sleep.

After the break we bowled tightly and professionally but without the penetration required to trouble the Pakistanis. They were behind the required run-rate for the first half of their innings, but still lost no wickets and it needed only a few successful speculative blows to swing the balance their way. Saadat Ali, one of their new-comers, supplied the necessary impetus with a series of wafting strokes which owed a good deal to fortune.

My own efforts were constantly hindered by a renewed no-ball epidemic. I am in almost as bad a state as I was in the 1980 home series against the West Indies, when every decent delivery was called. If I did manage to get my foot well behind the line the ball lobbed invitingly enough for the blade of Richards or Lloyd to dis-patch it to the boundary. At Old Trafford, I recall, Richards pun-ished me so severely that some of the media took it into their heads to report that he had a vendetta against me. The truth of it was I was bowling so badly he could hardly avoid taking me apart. Today the problem was great enough for me to have to resort to my fifteen-yard John Player League run-up; even off that, I contrived to over-step twice more. It is all the more worrying because there is no cricket in which I can sort it out away from the international scene. Getting it right in the nets is all very well but under match condi-tions I automatically strain that much more, which makes all the difference.

We managed to get rid of the top three Pakistanis, which raised brief hopes of a psychologically-inspired collapse at which they are rather adept. But Zaheer, still by a distance their best player, this time showed no nerves in playing a controlled and decisive innings at just the right pace. Helped by some uncharacteristically untidy fielding, Pakistan got home with eight balls to spare.

If that left us feeling deflated, worse was to come. On the injuries front, 'Flash' is now looking a doubtful starter for the Faisalabad Test because his groin has not responded to rest; but of even more moment is the news that Ian's knee injury has deteriorated suddenly and seriously. He had a good deal of trouble getting through his overs today and was virtually immobile in the field. The extent of the damage can be measured by the fact that in one slow-motion 'chase' into the outfield, even I beat him to the ball. Ian has suffered spasmodically with this complaint for years but it looks ominously as if it has collapsed on him this time. Bernard Thomas inspected it and agreed it was serious and I am afraid there must be a possibility that Ian will not complete the tour.

Our planned evening hosted by the British Embassy staff was convivial but, with so many problems buzzing around my head, could only be enjoyed to a limited degree. No sooner was I back in the hotel than A.C. called me to his room to discuss the latest outbreak of newspaper scandal. We hear that the *Daily Express* has a news team in New Zealand and *The Mail on Sunday* has two news writers here in Lahore. All of them are looking into the gutters, and it is at times such as this that my long-term reservations about the press turn to plain anger. We are not yet sure of the nature of their allegations, only that they seem intent on harassing the players and stirring up trouble.

There is talk that they are trying to pin a drugs scandal on certain

---

ENGLAND v PAKISTAN
Played at Lahore, 9 March 1984

Pakistan won by 6 wickets

ENGLAND 184 for 8 in 40 overs (A. J. Lamb 57, G. Fowler 43, Sarfraz Nawaz 3 for 33)

PAKISTAN 187 for 4 in 38.4 overs (Zaheer Abbas 59 not out, Saadat Ali 44, Mohsin Khan 39)

members of the side. Such rumours are not new – some, of a preposterous nature, reached us while we were still in New Zealand but nothing, to my knowledge, appeared in print. I wonder to what depths these new arrivals are about to stoop.

SATURDAY 10 MARCH There is no time to mope. Another Test begins on Monday and we have playing problems to solve.

In the nets, I worked for more than an hour on my most immediate concern but only reached the fairly obvious conclusion that bowling no-balls is a mental thing. It seems if my run-up dictates that I will land safely, far behind the line, something subconscious prevents me from letting the ball go in a properly aggressive manner – an interesting thought which gets me nowhere.

The tease of facing Qadir has been occupying several of our batsmen, none more so than Derek Randall, who today even invited a member of the press, an occasional purveyor of leg-spin, to bowl to him and try to simulate at least a degree of the problem. Until his tragic death during the West Indies tour three years ago, we always had dear old Kenny Barrington – no mean leg-spinner – to help out in such circumstances. Now, there is not an English leg-spinner in sight.

Ian Botham, of course, was in no state to practise. When we returned to the hotel he was with Bernard and the news was predictably bad. It was Bernard's opinion that nothing more could be done to patch him up out here; that he must go home to get quick and expert treatment, possibly involving surgery. Ever since our game at Palmerston North, where he twisted the knee on landing in a rough foothold, Ian has got by through having it strapped, and by dint of his unique, bullish determination. It is ironic that the only place he has ever missed a Test through illness is Pakistan, six years ago. Since then he has played sixty-five consecutive Tests, equalling the record, but it is Pakistan which has broken the run again. He will fly out tonight and be home sometime tomorrow. Sadly, cruelly, I fear the reporters who will inevitably meet him at Heathrow will not be concerned by his condition but will instead badger him with questions about drugs.

We now understand that *The Mail on Sunday* intends to name him in a claimed 'exposé'. Its two journalists have been here a couple of days and A.C. decided this afternoon that he should see them face to face and tell them that his own enquiries showed their

Abdul Qadir, the man uppermost in our minds throughout the Pakistan tour,
at home with his family in Lahore.

ABOVE AND LEFT After threats of student riots in Karachi, the authorities were taking no chances, as evidenced by the barbed-wire surrounds and the strong police presence. Thankfully, there were no such troubles this time around.

OPPOSITE

ABOVE Man of the match Abdul Qadir bowling his way through the England order; and at the end of a bouncer from yours truly during his frustrating knock of 40 in Pakistan's first innings at Karachi.

BELOW LEFT Azeem Hafeez, the left-arm seamer with three fingers missing from his right hand, with David Gower who marked a return to form with two fifties in the First Test.

BELOW RIGHT Nick Cook will remember the First Test with mixed feelings: he had the Pakistanis reeling in their first innings, only to drop Qadir at one, thus allowing Pakistan to build a healthy lead; and then nearly achieved the miracle with an inspired spell of bowling in Pakistan's second innings.

ABOVE A groundsman prepares the wicket – flat and unresponsive – for the Second Test at Faisalabad; and Graham Dilley takes out his frustration on it after seeing Salim Malik dropped off his bowling. Despite injury, he put up a spirited performance in this match and it's a tragedy that he will miss out on the whole of the 1984 season.

LEFT The impressive young Salim Malik, pick of the Pakistan batting with a fine century in the first innings and over 300 runs in the series.

OPPOSITE

ABOVE Wasim Raja, the second century-maker in Pakistan's first innings of 449 for eight declared.

BELOW LEFT AND RIGHT Stand-in captain David Gower (152), Mike Gatting (75); and Vic Marks (83) – three batsmen who prospered on the flat Faisalabad wicket during our match-saving 546 for eight declared.

ABOVE LEFT Graeme Fowler who, batting at number six, came to the rescue after we had plummeted to 83 for five in the first innings of the Lahore Test.

ABOVE RIGHT Bringing on the drinks during the morning of the second day at Lahore. Within forty-eight hours I was back in England with suspected hepatitis, utterly disorientated through following proceedings on the radio rather than being at the ground.

BELOW LEFT Having had Pakistan 181 for eight, victory seemed feasible – until man of the match Sarfraz (90) joined the injured Zaheer (82 not out) at the crease. Watching their stand while I was packing for home, it was not without its amusing moments.

BELOW RIGHT Having fallen from 175 for two to 189 for five, hopes of victory changed to fears of defeat. The rescue act came from David Gower (173 not out), dropped here by Mohsin Khan, and Vic Marks (55), so ending a fine series with the bat for both of them – Gower averaging 112 and Marks 43!

ABOVE Shoaib Mohammad (80), son of Hanif, and Mohsin Khan (104) during their record opening partnership of 173.

LEFT At 173 for no wicket, Pakistan required 70 to win off 14 overs. Norman Cowans (five for 42) broke the partnership and put in an inspired spell of bowling to save the game – a deserved slice of belated glory for a bowler who had worked hard on this tour.

RIGHT One of the *good* aspects of the tour was the continued development of Neil Foster, who kept cheerful when injured (by me) in New Zealand and then bowled his heart out in Pakistan.

allegations were a tissue of lies and fabrication. He wanted witnesses, however, in case the matter becomes a legal one and the paper claims we declined to deny the story. Norman Gifford and I were deputed for the unpleasant task. The issue is clearly a serious one and it does appear that things are stacking up against us in every way. To cap it all, I have begun to feel unwell. It is not just the usual problems one has to tolerate in Pakistan – the feeling that one can't leave the toilet for more than five minutes in any safety. I have a throbbing headache and stomach cramps so, after a visit to the team-room where Allan Lamb donned the 'Wally' suit for having forgotten his own home phone number, I went to bed, seeking sleep which would not come.

SUNDAY 11 MARCH I was still in bed at 9 a.m. when A.C. called. He told me it was best that I stayed there to try and summon the energy for the journey by road to Faisalabad. Bernard provided some tablets and I tried to doze, feeling dreadful. I could not face food and even packing my bags was a major effort.

At 11.30 I struggled downstairs to the business office the hotel provides for telex and telephone services. It is my wife Juliet's birthday and I wanted to phone her, but after ninety minutes of unsuccessful dialling I had to give up.

Lunch was a mistake. I forced myself to attempt some tomato soup and got through half an omelette before being sick. I boarded one of the three buses we had hired for the trip and lay on the back seat, my head on a pillow, my hands clutching my stomach. We had not travelled far when it became obvious that the bumpy road made that position impossibly uncomfortable, so I sat upright and stretched out my legs across the seat.

Gazing out of the window, the scenery was typical of the subcontinent. Small, bordered fields contained water buffalo and skinny, under-nourished goats. We passed through the occasional village, each with its stalls and its primitive Sunday market bartering. Then, right on cue, the coach broke down.

Black smoke belched from the engine into the cabin, making me feel still more nauseous. I had intended to stay on board but struggled off and sat down under the solitary tree available. Within twenty minutes, A.C. had decided that the repair job was a major one and that we would all have to squeeze into the space available on the other two buses.

It was four o'clock when our uncomfortable journey ended and we pulled up outside the Chenab Club, where we are to spend the week. It is, in many ways, an improvement on our worst fears. The rooms, for instance, are spotless, but the great drawback is that the club is situated on the main road and the noise is almost unbearable. The cacophony of rumbling trucks, scooters and hooters is not ideal for my pounding head.

The other lads went off to practise. I went to bed and tried to shut out the noise, aware that my chances of playing in tomorrow's Test are not great.

A.C. tells me that at least three papers have gone ahead and published their stories allegedly exposing the players' private lives in New Zealand. They will inevitably be damaging, to morale if not to reputation, but until we know the full details there is no more to be said. Grin and bear it if, on this awful evening, I could force a grin.

MONDAY 12 MARCH The rattle of an air-conditioner in an adjoining room woke me from a fitful, feverish doze. At half-past six I went down the corridor to tell the manager that I felt no better and would have to pull out of the game. Bernard appeared, gave me a cup of Bovril and told me to go back to my room and lie down. I attempted a few spoonfuls of baked beans, with no great relish, then 'Giff' and David Gower, who will take over the side, came in with A.C. to discuss strategy. We are effectively down to twelve players, which means one of the openers had to drop out. I could not put up much of a case for Tavaré playing, his net form remaining dire, so it was agreed that Fowler would play, though possibly in the middle-order to allow 'Gatt' to continue opening.

Most of the lads popped their heads round the door to tell me I look awful. They are, apparently, being well fed on provisions driven up each day from the Lahore Hilton and, although some of them are a little queasy and David Gower has a throat infection, their spirits remain high.

They disappeared to the ground and I settled down to the new experience of watching a Test match on television from my sick-bed. A.C. had kindly arranged for a set to be placed in my room and, after twiddling with the aerial for a while, I managed to establish a reasonable picture. When the telecast began I saw our lads taking the field, which meant we had lost the toss. I then saw 'Picca' deliver six no-balls in a protracted opening over – I thought I had troubles!

He was, however, bowling with some life and it was not long before he had Mohsin well caught in the gully by Lamb. 'Picca' then mysteriously left the field, and I felt frustrated lying here not knowing the reason.

'Lubo' brought on 'Beast'. The move worked, Mudassar quickly being caught off bat and pad by Gatting, who then took an even better catch at slip to dismiss Omar off Foster. Pakistan were 70 for three on what looked a very flat track and one more wicket at that stage might well have brought on an attack of the wobbles.

Our successes, however, dried up. Zaheer was reprieved when Gower dropped a rare catch, again off Foster, and proceeded to take the total to 200 in partnership with the impressive young Salim Malik. It was 'Gatt', almost a recognized partnership-breaker, who finally got through just after tea.

Zaheer was the man out, leg-before on the back foot, and if we had only possessed a relatively fresh seam bowler to attack the new batsman, Wasim Raja, we might have ended the day well. But 'Picca' was feeling under the weather – his ailment has been described as congestion on his chest – and 'Fozzy' was understandably weary. So the spinners were left to bowl out the final hour, Salim finishing unbeaten and in the nineties. Considering the fact that we lost the toss with three bowlers absent and another about to feel ill it was not as disastrous as it might have been.

When the team drifted back shortly after five, Bernard advised me to get up, shower and spend an hour or so in the team-room, if only so that I might feel more like sleeping when I returned to bed. It seemed a sensible idea but I felt so weak that it required a huge effort.

My bathroom is clean and neat but, standing under the shower and trying to adjust it for my height, it came away in my hand from its mounting on the wall. Such things only happen when you don't feel capable of doing anything about it.

Back in my room, not long afterwards, I ate two Ryvitas with honey and began to read a Dick Francis thriller.

TUESDAY 13 MARCH   The tablets have done their work in cementing me together, though I honestly can't imagine there is much left in my stomach. The staff at the club went to the trouble of making me some poached eggs and beans, so in order to avoid looking ungrateful I forced some down. When the blokes came in one by one it transpired that several now have bugs and bilious attacks of one kind or another, but none report the stomach cramps which, I am told, are the sign of something more severe. I certainly did not feel strong enough to venture out of bed for long.

The television cameras' view of the game has brought one or two things home to me, none more striking than the amount of good work done by Bob Taylor in terms of encouragement. I notice at the end of the over he frequently runs down to pat the bowler on the back and offer a few words. He must have been doing it a long time, I guess, but it is one of those things I fail to notice when I am concentrating on my own bowling and the side's progress.

It is increasingly clear that this game is being played on a pitch which should not produce a result. Pakistan made solid progress today, especially after surviving a lively and unlucky new-ball assault from Foster and Dilley. Poor 'Picca' bowled Salim with a real snorter, only to find the umpire calling no-ball again.

There was a power cut just before eleven so I had to resort to my portable radio to keep in touch with events. Salim was out before lunch for a very fine century and, when the players went off, I ate two more Ryvita biscuits.

Wasim Raja and Qadir got on top during the afternoon but I was pleased to see the lads were sticking to their task. The fielding was good and no heads were being allowed to drop. If one thing puzzled me it was the sparing use of Vic Marks's bowling – but then captaining a side, as I well know, is very much easier in front of a television set than on the field.

'Lubo' looked in at the end of the day for a few croaking words. His throat is worse and he reports that Dilley, Fowler and Lamb are all feeling rough. I managed to get myself up for another spell in the team-room, and felt more cheerful after taking two phone calls – one from Juliet, saying all was well at home, and another from 'Beefy', who is apparently going into hospital tomorrow. He didn't go into details about his reception from the press but A.C. showed me a copy of *The Mail on Sunday*. The first three pages of the paper are devoted to the drugs allegations and various other bits of scandal designed to titillate. Some of the innuendoes I found absolutely absurd, including one unsubstantiated allegation that certain players were smoking pot in the dressing-room at Christchurch during the Second Test, which we lost so humiliatingly. How anyone can honestly believe such a thing could have happened is completely beyond me, but I didn't feel like laughing about it.

My dinner was baked beans, Dundee cake and lots of the water we have imported. Then, while the boys sat down to watch *Bridge over the River Kwai* on the black and white video, I went back to bed, tried unsuccessfully to find World Service on my radio for any news of the Cheltenham race festival and settled instead for finishing off my book.

WEDNESDAY 14 MARCH Felt a bit better. Enjoyed the luxury of a shave. Managed breakfast. Life, in fact, seemed so much more worth living again that I asked Bernard if I could go to the ground. His view was that it would do me no harm but that I should not try to stay all day, so I decided to go down with the lads and return early.

My first sight of the Faisalabad ground since 1977 was a surprise. A new and luxurious pavilion has been built, with dressing-rooms to match anywhere in the world, but the ground was much smaller than I recalled. The memory can play tricks after six years.

While the usual warm-up routine went on without me, I read some English newspapers which the Embassy staff provided for us. All three of the 'heavies' – *Telegraph*, *Times* and *Guardian* – have been critical of my captaincy but, while it is not very pleasant to read, I have no complaints. Cricket writers are employed to give their views on such matters and it is certainly more valid a form of journalism than some we have suffered recently.

The match resumed. We set out with the primary target of 250 to avoid the follow-on and began well. Sitting out on the balcony in a deep arm-chair, I enjoyed the confidence of Gatting and Smith as they took us to lunch without alarms. And lunch – well, that was an amusing experience in itself, consisting of our own supplies of luncheon meat, corned beef and baked beans; an improvized feast, which some of the lads did not feel up to eating. I knew just what they were going through but persuaded all of them to get something down.

Our first setback came when 'Gatt' received a ball from Tauseef which bounced and turned, a most unlikely combination on this placid pitch. He was caught at short leg for 75 and, well as he had played, I have no doubt he is wondering why that first Test hundred remains so elusive.

So many of our batsmen were now affected by one illness or another that I had suggested to David that 'Arkle' should bat at number three. Not only had he managed to remain in ebullient health, but he was also unlikely to be so troubled by Qadir on a pitch with relatively little bounce. The move was agreed and, thankfully, worked well. Although we lost Smith before tea – dragging on a ball from Sarfraz via his boot – and Lamb in the last session – to a wild, firm-footed flash which he would not have played in better health – the day ended with us 233 for three, the follow-on all but dismissed from our minds and Randall still going well. Gower had joined him an hour before stumps, battling valiantly against the virus which had laid him low. Although there was no cricketing reason for us to have got into trouble on such a slow, flat pitch, it was encouraging to see everyone showing such spirit.

My own condition had improved so much that I was able to tackle my first proper meal in three days this evening. Tuesdays and Wednesdays in Pakistan are a bit restricted, menu-wise, as red meat is banned, so I had some chicken and rice and enjoyed it.

Back in the team-room, the social mafia of Marks and Fowler organized various games, including charades. I wondered fleetingly what the writers who have condemned our off-field behaviour would have made of this. After a long talk with some of the guys about England's recent overseas performances I went to bed, feeling a hundred percent better and actually looking forward to waking up. It had been a good evening – a flashback to the way touring had been on the sub-continent before the days of cassette players and videos.

THURSDAY 15 MARCH Rest day in Faisalabad. Whoopee! Woke up wondering how on earth we would pass the day.

After another breakfast of poached eggs and beans we soon resorted to the video, though this time I was all in favour. It was the last of the three episodes of *Minder* brought out by David Gower and, like the previous two, I found it hilarious entertainment. What a pity such a standard is the exception rather than the rule on British television.

Lunch was taken early, more for something to do than through any gnawing hunger. It was luncheon meat, and more beans. Then 'Lego' and myself were beaten on the club snooker table by messrs Gatting and Gower. I don't think Steve Davis has much to worry about from us. Back to the video for *Rollerball*, which I found pathetic but still watched because it passed a couple of hours.

Dinner was a very acceptable steak and kidney pie – the Lahore

Hilton have certainly looked after our evening meals in good style. When the video went on yet again this evening I retreated to the radio to listen to commentary on the Cheltenham Gold Cup. As Fifty Dollars More was unplaced, those bets struck with 'Beefy' and Alex Dibbs early in the tour are safe, which will help cheer up 'Giff', the latest health casualty.

Having run out of things to do I retired to bed at 9.30. It occurred to me that I had, unadventurously, not left the club compound all day. I am not sure I felt I'd missed anything, though.

FRIDAY 16 MARCH The trouble with going to bed at 9.30 in the evening is that I am awake again by 3.30. Outside my window, the traffic noise is relentless around the clock and further sleep was out of the question.

We left for the ground without Norman Gifford, who has a headache and stiff limbs, and Allan Lamb who has throat trouble. A lot of the other guys reported dizzy spells and stomach upsets of various kinds. It happens on every trip to Pakistan, but that knowledge is small consolation while it's happening to you.

With 'Giff' absent, I ran the net practice and tried to get some strength back into my legs just by walking around and fielding the ball. I am clearly still a long way from being fit enough to play in a game.

Although 'Arkle' was soon bowled through the 'gate' by Sarfraz, making an elementary mistake, we cruised past the follow-on mark. Fowler had gone in to join Gower and batted well, though I could not understand why Zaheer did not bowl the spinners against him early on, when he is plainly nervy against them. He lasted past lunchtime and had made 57 when he inexplicably tried to hit the leg-spinner over the top with a long-off posted deep, and paid the inevitable penalty.

We promoted Bob Taylor to number seven as, in Karachi, he had played Qadir much more comfortably than Vic Marks. But the best-laid plans . . . he was caught off bat and pad for nought and 'Skid' had to come in anyway. He was initially uncertain and ungainly, lunging at the ball when Qadir brought him forward. But, as confidence grew, he began to let the ball come on to the bat. He survived and then prospered, and his stand with the admirable Gower should ensure that we do not lose this Test.

The partnership was punctuated by two 'Oscar' performances.

Qadir, who is naturally theatrical when bowling, produced one of his most prolonged dancing, pleading appeals for a bat-pad catch against Gower; then Sarfraz upstaged him with an extraordinary display when Marks missed a hook against a short ball. He refused to accept the not-out verdict for his caught-behind appeal and strode across to consult the square-leg umpire. Nick Cook wittily suggested he must have been checking that the ball carried – it in fact reached the keeper at head height.

Gower was never in any great trouble and, having studied the pitch this morning, I can see why. It is a much more resilient surface than the Karachi Test pitch and even on this fourth day there is no sign of cracks widening or crumbling. A player of Gower's class certainly should make runs here and, after his desperately lean time in New Zealand, it is good to see him back in form with the bat. He has followed his two fifties in Karachi with a century here and, as both he and 'Skid' are still there tonight, we have a first-innings lead with four wickets in hand – a healthy position to take into the last day. There may not be much chance of a victory but then that was always unlikely on this wicket. We must just hope for slightly more responsive conditions and a chance to square the series in Lahore.

The lads were rightly happy tonight, both about the state of the game and the fact that this was their final evening in Faisalabad. The locals have done everything possible to make us welcome and conditions here are nowhere near as bad as I recall from previous visits. But illness has still struck pretty widely and, combined with the sheer boredom of the free time, it means everyone will be glad to move on.

SATURDAY 17 MARCH Downed my last lot of poached eggs and beans, then took my cricket kit case to the ground for the first time, on the final day of the game. I had a gentle bowl off three or four paces in the nets, my first exertions for a week, but my legs still feel weak and wobbly. With the final Test starting on Monday I am beginning to run out of time to convince myself, and the rest of the selectors, that I have recovered sufficiently to get through it.

The sun does not often shine with complete conviction here and today, as usual, an industrial haze covered the city so that, if one could ignore the temperature, it might easily have been an overcast day at Old Trafford.

ENGLAND v PAKISTAN
Second Test

Played at Iqbal Stadium, Faisalabad, 12, 13, 14, 16, 17 March 1984
Match drawn

Pakistan

Mohsin Khan c Lamb b Dilley	20	– b Dilley	2
Mudassar Nazar c Gatting b Cook	12	– lbw b Foster	4
Qasim Omar c Gatting b Foster	16	– c Taylor b Dilley	17
Salim Malik c Lamb b Cook	116	– c sub (N. G. Cowans) b Marks	76
*Zaheer Abbas lbw b Gatting	68	– not out	32
Wasim Raja b Marks	112	– not out	5
Abdul Qadir c Foster b Dilley	50		
†Anil Dalpat lbw b Dilley	8		
Sarfraz Nawaz not out	16		
Tauseef Ahmed not out	1		
Azeem Hafeez did not bat			
L-b 11, w 2, n-b 17	30	L-b 1	1

1/35 2/53 3/70 4/200   (8 wkts dec.) 449   1/6 2/6 3/56 4/123   (4 wkts) 137
5/323 6/416 7/430 8/433

Bowling: *First Innings*—Foster 30–7–109–1; Dilley 28–6–101–3; Cook 54–14–133–2; Marks 27–9–59–1; Gatting 3–0–17–1. *Second Innings*—Dilley 9–0–41–2; Foster 5–1–10–1; Cook 16–6–38–0; Marks 8–2–26–1; Gatting 2–0–18–0; Fowler 1–0–3–0.

England

C. L. Smith b Sarfraz	66
M. W. Gatting c Salim b Tauseef	75
D. W. Randall b Sarfraz	65
A. J. Lamb c Anil b Hafeez	19
*D. I. Gower st Anil b Mudassar	152
G. Fowler c Omar b Wasim	57
†R. W. Taylor c Salim b Qadir	0
V. J. Marks b Sarfraz	83
G. R. Dilley not out	2
N. G. B. Cook not out	1
N. A. Foster did not bat	
B 10, l-b 4, n-b 12	26

1/127 2/163 3/214 4/245   (8 wkts dec.) 546
5/361 6/361 7/528 8/545

Bowling: *First Innings*—Hafeez 19–3–71–1; Sarfraz 50–11–129–3; Wasim 26–6–61–1; Qadir 51–14–124–1; Tauseef 30–8–96–1; Mudassar 13–1–39–1.

Man of the Match: D. I. Gower

Umpires: Javed Akhtar and Mahboob Shah.

In competitive terms the day was always likely to be of only academic interest – and so it proved. But we certainly made the running and emerged with the positive end of a draw, our confidence renewed for the last Test of the tour.

Zaheer set defensive fields from the start for Mudassar and Sarfraz. When Qadir came on he was unable to obtain any bounce and was played with some authority by both Gower and Marks. When 'Lubo' was finally out for 152, stumped trying a big hit off Mudassar, 'Skid' took the initiative until Sarfraz bowled him for a very fine 83.

We declared at lunch, 97 ahead, and although both Lamb and Smith were not well enough to take the field, the blokes went out positively to try for a miracle. Graham Dilley bowled splendidly. It has not been a great tour for him, dogged by injury and loss of confidence, but today he was very quick on a slow wicket and he rapidly dismissed Mohsin through sheer pace. Foster had Mudassar leg-before, playing across the line, and when David brought 'Picca' back for a second spell, his first delivery accounted for the stocky Qasim Omar. Zaheer then looked very unhappy as Dilley charged in at him: just momentarily, I felt Pakistan were teetering on the brink of another panic.

Salim Malik, however, is a cool customer and for the second time in the match he cut short our ambitions of causing complete collapse. A lot of us believe he is one of the most impressive batting newcomers in world cricket, playing very straight and with enormous confidence. By the time he was caught off 'Skid', the game had long since passed into *Wisden* as a stalemate.

David Gower was a well-deserved man of the match. While he collected the award and dealt with the end-of-game interviews which would normally be my responsibility, I was myself standing in for poor 'Giff' by organizing the dispatch of our baggage.

With much chivvying up, we were on board the buses and away by just after 4.30, aiming to reach Lahore in daylight. They were modern, comfortable mini-buses but the ride was still bumpy and, at times, hair-raising. We crawled through congested traffic on the outskirts of Lahore and the welcome sight of the Hilton loomed up at twenty past seven. I found myself in the same room as I had occupied last week and, while unpacking, peered out of the window at the rare sight of a spectacular thunderstorm. If the weather is turning nasty it may be yet another enemy to our chances of levelling the score in the series.

9

AN EARLY RETURN HOME

SUNDAY 18 MARCH The storm has done its worst. A.C. went off to the ground before most of the lads were out of bed this morning and returned to report that a morning practice was impossible. The net wicket was a strip of mud and the outfield had pools of water on it. There was no option but to delay our session until after lunch but it was an unwanted irritant, especially as I was so badly in need of some work to build up strength.

'Picca' came to see me and said he was very worried about a lack of feeling up his right leg. This has been troubling him for a while, to a lesser degree, but after his bowling yesterday he now says he has no sensation above his waistline, either. Not liking the sound of it at all, I spoke to Bernard Thomas who agreed to summon a local doctor.

Lunchtime arrived. The lads were sitting around the hotel, restless, when I joined A.C. on another pitch-reconnaissance mission. We looked at three possible practice grounds but eventually decided the Gymkhana ground was the driest. As I needed a bowl, I went there straightway with Bob Taylor, the others following just for a loosening run and some catching practice.

Bowling was hard work. I got through the equivalent of four overs then had to rest, the power gone from my legs and lungs. I tried another burst but things just felt progressively worse. A.C., who was watching, advised me to stop rather than kill myself. Stubbornly, I argued that I could not go into a Test without a decent work-out, but eventually I had to see sense. I moved across to join the fielding session and hit some catches for twenty minutes. After that I felt totally drained and, although some of the blokes ran back to the hotel, it was as much as I could do to clamber on the mini-bus.

More bad news awaited me at the hotel. Bernard told me that Picca's condition was causing great concern and that the doctor had insisted there was no possibility of him playing tomorrow. Apparently, it is possible to stick a pin in his leg without any sign of reaction. Sorry as we are to lose him, especially after his good efforts at Faisalabad, he must go home for specialist advice. A flight to London via Karachi was arranged for him, and I went off to the bath thinking the fates had turned against us again.

The selectors are virtually redundant. We now have only thirteen players left, of whom Tavaré will again be the omitted batsman. The final bowling place will depend entirely on how I shape up in the morning. At tonight's team meeting I expressed delight at the Faisalabad performance, commented on one or two things I had noticed while watching on television, then handed over to David Gower to chair further discussion.

We spoke in great detail about how we should bowl to Salim, Zaheer and Qadir, who have caused us most trouble with the bat. Mudassar has been dropped, along with Tauseef and Azeem, and by bringing in two new batsmen they have made it very clear they intend to take no chances. They will bat down to number nine with competent players and it is going to be very hard work bowling them out twice.

MONDAY 19 MARCH Poor old A.C. must live in fear of the telephone ringing. His latest call from London was to tell him that Ian Botham has apparently stepped out of line by making derogatory remarks about Pakistan during a BBC radio interview. I talked it over with the manager at breakfast: if 'Beefy' said all the things attributed to him it is completely uncalled for. His conclusion, apparently, is that England should not have to tour here because conditions are so bad, yet the hotels in Karachi and Lahore have been first class on this visit and even at Faisalabad (where Ian did not go) the Chenab Club was perfectly adequate if not luxurious. Most of the illnesses we have suffered seem to have been the result of an infectious bug and have little or nothing to do with the food. This sort of thing only adds to our pile of problems.

To depress me further, I was clearly not fit enough to play. Yesterday's efforts had resulted in me feeling even shakier this morning and, although I left the decision as late as possible, I knew in my heart it was hopeless. When we got to the ground I took Bob Taylor on to the outfield and bowled twelve deliveries into his gloves before my heavy breathing and unsteady legs forced me to rest. A five-day game was out of the question, so I wasted no time and told 'Lubo' he would be in charge again.

After a look at the pitch, which was a little two-toned after the rains but seemed to be firm even on the dark parts, I spoke to 'Foxy', who wanted to know why he was batting at six instead of opening. The reasons were twofold. Gatting and Smith had done well as a pair at Faisalabad and when Fowler last played he had made fifty at number six. He went away placated.

We wanted to bat first so it was a pleasant surprise when Zaheer won the toss and put us in. We were not so joyful about it three hours later when five wickets had gone down for 83, but the pitch was in no way to blame for that. Conditions were ideal for batting and a commanding position was ours for the taking, yet somehow we contrived to make a mess of it again. It was a tragedy to lose so many wickets on this of all occasions, because Pakistan had crowded so many batsmen into their line-up that their bowling attack was thin and largely inexperienced. The bowling burden fell heavily on the shoulders of Sarfraz and Qadir, and as Qadir had confided this morning that even he was suffering with dizziness and headaches I had been full of hope that we would cash in.

I am afraid most of the wounds were self-inflicted. Gatting was playing across the line when Sarfraz had him leg-before; Gower played a dreadful waft at the new seamer, Mohsin Kamal, and was caught behind; and Smith, having played soundly for some time, was not to the pitch of the ball when he edged Sarfraz to second slip; Lamb then succumbed to his increasingly familiar defensive failing and gave a bat-pad catch. When Randall was adjudged caught somewhat questionably at silly-point, I could scarcely believe the plight in which we found ourselves.

As if to mock us for this wretchedly timed collapse, Pakistan even lost their captain, Zaheer taking no further part after injuring his groin in the field. Sarfraz, whose influence on this series has been considerable for one who seems to have been finished in Test cricket as often as me, took over as skipper with some relish but his plans for further advances were foiled by our Social Mafia. Marks and Fowler played quite splendidly to put on over 100 and heaven knows what the consequences might have been if one of these two had got out early. As it was, 'Skid' batted through almost to stumps before 'walking' for a bat-pad decision which the umpire looked like giving in his favour. We were 241 for nine at the close, not a great platform for victory, and once more we were talking of what went wrong.

The serious part of the evening involved an informal chat by the management on the state of English cricket. We all agreed that the game we play in England is not suited to producing Test players and that, since the flood of one-day competitions and Championship bonus points, batting talent has been submerged and destroyed by the constant need to adapt.

The funny part of the evening was the 'Wally' award. It was Bernard Thomas tonight, which presented our long-serving physiotherapist with something of a problem as he had made arrangements to go to a local performance of *The Merchant of Venice* by a travelling theatre company from England. Not being permitted to shed his own costume, he had no option but to wear the brown shirt, yellow tie and hat in the stalls.

When I went to bed at the scandalously late hour of 9.15 I made the mistake of looking at my profile, stripped, in the mirror. This illness has obviously been a debilitating business because I have lost a lot of weight off my chest and thighs and really don't look like an athlete of any description right now.

TUESDAY 20 MARCH   After bowling off three paces for a while and still feeling shockingly weak, I asked Bernard Thomas if he could find a doctor to examine me. I went to the local hospital after lunch and the doctor told me he thought my condition was the result of loss of fluid in hot weather. This certainly seems to happen every time I come to the sub-continent, and sometimes in other hot climates. He took a blood test, which I was pleased to have just in case it showed anything positive.

Back at the ground we were having a good day. Although we had lost our last wicket without addition this morning – and 241 did not look a great total to defend – 'Flash' and 'Fozzy' bowled so well with the new ball that we were soon on top. They each had a very confident lbw shout rejected but, keeping a good line and generating a lively pace, they soon had both the openers out leg-before. I thought the field-placings were mostly very good. We had talked before the match about sacrificing third man and blocking off the mid-off area where we seemed to have conceded a lot of runs. This worked pretty well. Eight or nine runs might have been scored through the vacant third man region but we generally looked tighter than of late.

Qasim Omar, short and wristy, and Salim Malik, taller and more orthodox, put on 86 for the third wicket at rather less than two runs an over before Salim, who had earlier been dropped at slip by 'Gatt', was bowled by Vic Marks. We then kept things very tight until tea and made significant headway in the final session. Foster took two more wickets, Omar and Ramiz Raja both swatting ineptly at short balls, and when Cowans returned he had Wasim Raja caught at gully, fending a sharply rising delivery off his nose.

Frustrated as I am to be confined to the pavilion, I was very heartened today by the spirited performance in the field and it certainly bodes well for the future to see our two young seamers getting batsmen out through pace and hostility. As Zaheer is badly hampered by his groin injury and has a runner, we may well be in an even better position than the score of 171 for six would suggest. It only goes to emphasize that we have here two mediocre batting sides, because there should be no excuses for failure on this pitch.

Cheered psychologically by events on the field, I felt strong enough to visit the hotel's main restaurant for the first time tonight, eating with Graeme Fowler and Vic Marks to discuss the make-up of the end-of-tour party.

WEDNESDAY 21 MARCH My tour is over. The doctor from Lahore General Hospital arrived just after eleven this morning and advised me to sit down. He then said I had jaundice. I pressed him for more details and he explained he suspects a mild form of hepatitis, which took me completely by surprise. Although I was aware my condition was something more severe than flu, we had been innoculated against hepatitis before leaving New Zealand so I had never considered it as a possibility.

A.C., who has had the disease, was full of anxiety and, when the doctor said I would need a month in bed followed by six months off alcohol, it was soon clear I would not get the necessary rest here. Going home was the last thing I wanted to do but A.C. and Bernard convinced me it was the only sensible course to take and immediately put the wheels in motion to find me a flight back. As the British Ambassador was present at the game, he was able to help and I was soon told that I would be going to Rawalpindi tonight, then returning to London on a British Airways flight early tomorrow morning.

The lads were told at lunchtime of my departure and there were plenty of comic cracks about the twelve-man tour party, which is what they will now be. Shortly after the break I was driven back to the hotel to pack my bags. It had all happened so fast – and the worst of it is I now feel better than I have done since falling ill.

While I went about the duties of packing, sending a telex to Lord's and trying to warn my wife by phone, I kept an eye on the cricket on television. The day had begun promisingly for us, 'Fozzy' taking two more wickets to have Pakistan 181 for eight. This completed Foster's first five-wicket haul in Test cricket and I could not be more pleased. When we arrived in Pakistan I had a wager with him that his Test bowling average would still be above 60 at the end of the tour. It was struck partly to motivate him, partly because I could not honestly see him getting much response from the pitches here. I am delighted to have been proved wrong.

Sarfraz joined his limping captain Zaheer and we were entitled to look forward to a first-innings lead. The lads on the field clearly believed Sarfraz was out caught behind for single figures, but the exaggerated reactions of Foster, the bowler, and of Bob Taylor, though understandable, could still not be condoned. When Sarfraz then survived an equally confident lbw shout, I began to fear that the initiative was slipping away – and so it proved.

The pair were still together when I switched on the television back at the hotel, still together when I finished my packing, and still together when I returned to the room after managing at length to get through to Juliet on the phone. This last time, however, I was greeted by the unfamiliar sight of C. L. Smith bowling and, in the great tradition of the partnership-breaking occasional bowler, he immediately had Sarfraz caught at slip by Gatting. Sarfraz, however, had made 90, his highest Test score by a distance, and it could hardly have been made at a worse time for us. Mohsin Kamal was out straightway, Zaheer remained undefeated on 82, and the Pakistanis led by 102.

Splitting my concentration between the screen and the dozens of essential jobs which suddenly spring to mind an hour before you must leave for home, I saw us lose two wickets, took solace in the sturdy resistance of Gower and Gatting and felt that 65 for two – 37 runs behind – was neither promising nor desperate.

I had set up camp in the team-room. One by one, the lads came in to say goodbye. I tried to give each of them a word or two of thanks and encouragement but it was the type of occasion when it seemed impossible to choose the right thing to say – I felt so disappointed at having to leave them.

A.C. saw me off on my drive to the airport, where I was ushered into the VIP lounge and filled in time reading my Sidney Sheldon novel until the plane took off for Islamabad. I had been booked into a hotel but Mark Lyall-Grant of the Embassy staff met me and offered me a room at his house. Having pointed out that all I wanted to do was go to bed, I gratefully accepted and, while Mark went off to play darts, I retired for the night shortly after ten.

THURSDAY 22 MARCH At five o'clock, Mark's bearer hammered on my door. I showered, dressed and came down for breakfast, which included the first bacon I have tasted in weeks. It was a pleasant drive to the airport, arrangements were smooth and the kind people here had pulled strings so that I could travel back in the comfort of a first-class seat. Even though I had to resist the fine wines being proferred, and felt no great appetite for the good food, I was very grateful for the space and the seclusion.

The film was the same John Travolta 'epic' I had studiously avoided on the flight into Pakistan. I did the same again, concentrating on classical music through the headphones and vague thoughts about the strength of the press reception for me. I knew A.C. had requested they should leave me alone but I was well aware the request would be ignored.

We landed at Heathrow shortly before 5 p.m. and Peter May, chairman of selectors, was among the welcoming party. So were innumerable cameramen and a few reporters. I was ushered rapidly through them all to the car park, where Juliet was waiting, and I was in the passenger seat of my car and away before I realized there had been no time to thank Peter for coming to meet me.

Through the rush hour, across north London suburbia and on to the M1-M6 route back to Birmingham, where I found one particularly persistent pressman waiting in my road. I told him briefly there was no chance of an interview, then went indoors for my first view of our daughter. She looked peaceful and content. I felt tired and listless. She was already in bed. I rapidly did the same.

FRIDAY 23 MARCH My introduction to the cares of parenthood. Juliet was up for the day's first feed at 3.30 a.m. I dozed only fitfully afterwards before getting up for a soothing session of Wagner before my doctor's appointment at nine o'clock.

He told me that whatever I had contracted was not infectious so

ENGLAND v PAKISTAN
Third Test

Played at Gaddafi Stadium, Lahore, 19, 20, 21, 23, 24 March 1984
Match drawn

England

C. L. Smith c Salim b Sarfraz.................18 – (2) run out........................... 15
M. W. Gatting lbw b Sarfraz................. 0 – (3) run out........................... 53
*D. I. Gower c Anil b Mohsin Kamal........ 9 – (4) not out.....................173
A. J. Lamb c Ramiz b Qadir.................29 – (5) c & b Qadir..................... 6
D. W. Randall c Salim b Qadir.............14 – (6) c Salim b Qadir.............. 0
G. Fowler c Omar b Qadir....................58 – (1) c Anil b Mohsin Kamal...... 19
V. J. Marks c Mohsin Khan b Qadir........74 – c sub (Akram Raza) b Qadir...... 55
†R. W. Taylor lbw b Sarfraz................. 1 – (10) b Sarfraz 5
N. A. Foster lbw b Qadir...................... 6 – (8) lbw b Qadir.................... 0
N. G. B. Cook c Anil b Sarfraz................. 3
N. G. Cowans not out........................ 3 – (9) st Anil b Qadir................. 3
B 4, l-b 5, w 9, n-b 8 26	B 6, l-b 3, w 1, n-b 5 ... 15

1/5 2/20 3/47 4/77   241   1/35 2/38 3/175   (9 wkts dec.) 344
5/83 6/203 7/205 8/222 9/237   4/189 5/189 6/308 7/309 8/327
                                  9/344

Bowling: *First Innings*—Mohsin Kamal 15-0-66-1; Sarfraz 22.5-5-49-4; Qadir 30-7-84-5; Wasim 11-4-16-0. *Second Innings*—Mohsin Kamal 17-3-59-1; Sarfraz 27.4-1-112-1; Qadir 42-5-110-5; Wasim 21-5-48-0.

Pakistan

Mohsin Khan lbw b Foster.................... 1 – c Smith b Cowans.................104
Shoaib Mohammad lbw b Cowans........... 7 – c Gatting b Cowans.............. 80
Qasim Omar c Fowler b Foster.............73 – run out 0
Salim Malik b Marks........................38 – c Gatting b Cowans.............. 7
Ramiz Raja c Smith b Foster.................26 – (8) not out........................ 6
Wasim Raja c Gower b Cowans.............12 – lbw b Cowans 0
*Zaheer Abbas not out.........................82 – (5) c Gatting b Cowans........... 5
Abdul Qadir c Taylor b Foster............. 3
†Anil Dalpat c Gower b Foster............. 2
Sarfraz Nawaz c Gatting b Smith...........90 – (7) not out........................ 10
Mohsin Kamal c Gower b Cook............. 0
L-b 9 9	L-b 5........................ 5

1/9 2/13 3/99 4/138   343   1/173 2/175 3/187   (6 wkts) 217
5/151 6/166 7/175 8/181 9/342   4/197 5/199 6/199

Bowling: *First Innings*—Cowans 29-5-89-2; Foster 32-8-67-5; Cook 46-12-117-1; Marks 20-4-59-1; Smith 1-0-2-1. *Second Innings*—Cowans 14-2-42-5; Foster 15-4-44-0; Cook 18.3-2-73-0; Marks 10-0-53-0; Smith 1-1-0-0.

Man of the Match: Sarfraz Nawaz

Umpires: Amanullah Khan and Khizar Hayat.

there ought to be no danger to Juliet or Katie-Anne. He had, however, fixed an appointment for me at the Tropical Diseases Hospital for tomorrow.

Yesterday having been the rest day in Lahore, I was able to pick up the Test again almost uninterrupted. It was an odd sensation – listening on the radio to a match several thousand miles away in which, circumstances being a little different, I would have been playing.

'Gatt' and 'Lubo' had been playing well for some while. Then came a forty-minute break in the line and, while Radio Three filled in with music and chat, we managed to lose three rapid wickets. The rescue act came from 'Skid' Marks, valiantly supporting David in a stand which should have staved off the threat of defeat. Sadly, that afternoon collapse stifled the acceleration just as we had begun to look for a declaration and it would seem from this distance that a draw is now the most we can hope for.

During the afternoon I invested a little cash on the televized racing, having consulted Ian Botham by telephone about the prospects of his horse, Rely on Guy, at Doncaster. It was a wholly fruitless wager. The horse finished last.

I went through the pile of mail which had built up during my three absent months – it never ceases to amaze me how many people write when it would seem to be pretty widely known I am out of the country – and then took a welcome commiseratory call from Elton John in Sydney. By 9 p.m. I was whacked. By 9.30 I was asleep in bed.

SATURDAY 24 MARCH Play had just resumed in Lahore when I woke – but it was 10 a.m. there, only 5 a.m. in Birmingham. I kept in touch with the match via TV's Teletext service until the live commentary began after lunch, delighting in the continued good form of Vic Marks and the comments of those on the radio who had so recently been ridiculing his batting. Gower, meanwhile, went on to 173 not out. The figures speak for themselves. When he is in form, there is no better player in the world. He then declared, challenging Pakistan to score 243 in 59 overs.

At ten o'clock I was seated in the consulting rooms of my Scottish specialist, discussing the history and progression of this virus which seems to affect me so severely in hot climates. He told me my liver was enlarged but that, after studying the blood analysis from Pakistan, it was his view I did not have hepatitis. He was, however, very keen that I should rest entirely, putting myself under no pressure, mental or physical. I also had to stay off alcohol – not that up to now I feel like drinking any. I gave what Tony Hancock would no doubt have called 'an armful of blood' and was asked to come back for the result of the tests next Friday.

When I left the surgery, Pakistan were 170 without loss and we looked doomed. But if there was an undoubted gamble involved in the declaration, there was also a certain logic, because Pakistan are well known for their tendency to panic when victory is near, as we experienced so agonizingly in the First Test at Karachi. This time it manifested itself later in the innings, but no less dramatically. As soon as they lost one wicket, more followed. 'Flash' Cowans bowled an inspired spell and, from the commentary, it sounded as if Mike Gatting could do nothing wrong. Of the first four wickets to fall, he caught three and ran out the other.

Suddenly the initiative was with us and, although the game ended predictably in a draw, we had come out of it well. I was relieved and delighted for everyone, but especially for 'Flash', who has worked hard on the trip and deserves this slice of belated glory.

I listened to every ball, through to the end. I also listened to some scathing criticism of myself and could not pretend it didn't hurt. They were chewing me up, hammering my captaincy as 'painful to watch', praising David Gower's performance in, creditably, reducing Pakistan to 217 for six as a masterpiece and choosing to overlook my own earlier efforts in having them 66 for seven in Karachi. I suppose I should not be upset any more, certainly not surprised. It has been obvious for some while that the media have been thirsting for a new captain, as they periodically do, and that they would tear me apart as soon as the excuse arose.

I watched the racing on *Grandstand*, marvelling at the artistry of flat jockey Steve Cauthen and the resilience of jumping champion John Francome, who is under the extraordinary threat of a newspaper eager to release tapes culled from a scandalous tapping of his phone – the depths to which newspapers will stoop for a story never fails to astound me. Turned the clocks forward and staggered to bed at 9.30, still tired and weak.

SUNDAY 25 MARCH Wonder how the guys are filling in their final rest day in Pakistan. Expect the leather shop in Karachi will be getting some custom and that the last rays of sun around the hotel swimming pool will have been soaked up. Feel absolutely sure they are all ready for home. It's been a taxing, troubled tour in many ways.

The phone was busy today with calls from various friends but I ventured no further than my chair in front of the television, where I sat through soccer and ice-skating: felt excited by neither and turned back to my music. Still no appetite.

MONDAY 26 MARCH The final one-day international carried no radio commentary so I could only follow the game through the hourly news bulletins. Heard about some crowd unrest and hoped, at this last stage of the tour, it would not amount to much. Heard Pakistan had been restricted to only 163 for eight in forty overs, thanks mainly to the improbable bowling success of messrs Gatting and Smith. Then, as I lay on the sofa, snoozing between bulletins, I heard our fairly comfortable progress to a six-wicket win and a satisfying conclusion to the tour. Thought of the lads drifting back to the welcoming cool and luxury of the Holiday Inn from the heat and dust of the National Stadium, packing their cricket bags and gathering for their final team meeting. Wished I could have been with them to the end. Fell into a restless sleep.

ENGLAND v PAKISTAN
Played at Karachi, 26 March 1984

England won by 6 wickets

PAKISTAN 163 for 8 in 40 overs (Saadat Ali 78 not out, Mohsin Khan 37, M. W. Gatting 3 for 32)

ENGLAND 164 for 4 in 38.4 overs (M. W. Gatting 38 not out, D. I. Gower 31)

10

REFLECTIONS

It was a Friday in Faisalabad, and I was beginning to feel life might be tolerable again after the worst days of my illness, when I picked up a recent copy of the London *Daily Telegraph*, turned to the leader page and plunged straight back to my most morbid thoughts.

I was not sure whether the piece which had caught my eye was trying to be clever or merely sarcastic, or whether the writer really did believe he was making a valid point. What I did know was that it was completely unfair and it left me feeling very bitter.

The tone of this masterpiece of editorial comment was ironic chastisement of yours truly for allegedly having made so many different excuses for England's defeats. It was claimed I had blamed the pitches, umpiring, injuries, itinerary, travelling and conditions, among other things, and the writer concluded that 'a period of silence is called for'.

'Never let the facts get in the way of a good story' is the oldest jokey cliché of Fleet Street but it would appear to hold some truth. At the point in question, I had uttered one complaint on tour – about certain pitches in New Zealand. I had deliberately said nothing about umpires, had stated the facts of injuries without embellishment, had pointed out that the itinerary had been tailored to meet players' wishes and had nothing but praise for travel and conditions. Yet here I was, branded a whingeing pom. It was something I could have done without, especially bearing in mind my original reluctance to pamper the travelling press with too many conferences. Having fallen in line with official wishes and given interviews at all the customary times it was more than a little galling to find my co-operation being greeted in at least one corner of Fleet Street with such scornful resentment.

Perhaps I should not have been surprised or upset. When a sporting team is beaten, the world awaits the captain's excuses. Those who have reached this point of my book may expect a whitewash job and a claim that we were robbed only by a conspiracy of circumstances. The fact is, we were not. We lost the series to New Zealand and Pakistan because we are not a very good team; and because we performed disastrously below even our acceptable standards for three or four critical sessions in Test matches.

Of course there were problems – unusual outside pressures, too, particularly towards the end of the tour when we seemed barely to have survived one crisis when another confronted us. But the crux of our problem was plain and simple. We just weren't good enough.

It may sound a damning indictment of English cricket when we have to admit we were not capable of beating New Zealand and Pakistan, previously such Test match also-rans, but the game has changed dramatically. Only the West Indies have managed to win series away from home in recent years and I would currently rate them and Australia head and shoulders above the other countries on ability. It is hard to win on tour, where everything is by definition more familiar and friendly to the home team, and New Zealand, Pakistan, India and ourselves have all been faring badly.

Having said that, I still won't accept that, man for man, we are not a better side than New Zealand. It was the defeat there which disappointed me most of all because we had one chance to win, failed to take it and then surrendered the series with a performance at Christchurch which would have shamed even a club team.

I hate to trot out the old, clichéd reasons for failure and I am sure the batsmen will resent shouldering the burden of blame from me, a bowler. But the fact is that, despite playing on four very good pitches out of the six provided for Tests, our batting was painfully brittle. Derek Randall was outstanding in New Zealand, David Gower was brilliant in Pakistan and Chris Smith turned in the type of workmanlike results I had expected of him. But the form and figures of the rest were not pleasant to view.

In their defence, English batsmen are accustomed to playing four or five innings a week, getting into a groove and never feeling rusty. On this tour that was not possible – some of them went several weeks at a time without playing a single competitive innings. No matter how hard one practises, there is no substitute for match conditions.

Watching our batsmen in the nets was frequently a depressing experience. Neil Foster, for example, would bowl at a variety of batters over a period of an hour and, if anyone had been keeping tally, I suspect he would have emerged with figures of something like seven for 20. Most of the batsmen were getting 'out' four or five times in a twenty-minute net – and it was not through casualness. They were simply in such poor form that they were being bowled, trapped leg-before and edging the ball almost as many times as they middled it. I stated during the diary that I had never seen so many batsmen out of form on a tour and it is worth repeating in hindsight. On every tour, I confidently expect two of the front-line batsmen to fail completely. On this tour, there were never more than two who were in form! Their confidence was low and it would have been reckless to go into a Test with only six batsmen. So we usually played seven and then, as in Wellington, found that we could not make the most of a winning position because we had only four bowlers.

There are a number of reasons for such batting doldrums but the basic problem lies in shortage of technique and absence of competition. I believe the technical shortcomings are a direct result of one-day cricket and the English player's constant need to adapt his style to suit the length of game. Other than Gower and Ian Botham, whose God-given talent is plain for all to see, all those who have learned the game since the advent of the John Player League in 1969 are not technically correct enough to prosper consistently in Test cricket. There is a counter-argument which I have heard expressed by Alan Knott. He says that Tests have never been so exciting as they are nowadays because the ball is almost always on top of the bat; the chances of a match like the Old Trafford Test of 1964, when England and Australia each scored 600-plus and the third innings was hardly begun, have contracted drastically. I accept the point, accept even that the average spectator would rather see a few wickets falling than have the bat in complete command. But I fear our standards have fallen too far.

Competition for places has been lacking in the batting department. The seven batsmen we took on tour are, in my opinion, far and away the best players in England. They may not have produced the results to back my judgement, but try to pick an alternative batting order and you will soon find you are among very ordinary county players. This is, in itself, an unhealthy situation because it inevitably breeds complacency – probably not wilful and perhaps not even conscious – among those whose places are relatively safe: no one who feels himself free of pressure for his job will produce his best all the time.

I would not criticise the players' approach to practice. In fact, apart from on the odd occasion, I have never seen a touring side practise so conscientiously. But I cannot pretend that everything is as it should be off the field. My main concern lies not with the much-publicized social excesses we are accused of committing but with the mental resilience of the players to the undisguised drudgery which touring can sometimes become. It annoys me sometimes when too rosy a picture is painted of tour life, too glamorous an image conjured in the mind of the starry-eyed young professional. It isn't like that at all. Sure, there are good times, exciting times, amusing times, and I am not saying I would swap my career for anyone else's. But in any job which involves a good deal of travelling, the glamour is only skin-deep. I see air crews scratching one another's eyes out after a fortnight away, businessmen bored and irritable after a three-day trip. Cricketers are away for a minimum of three months every winter and, everyone being different, some adjust to the false hotel life much more readily than others. Many of the younger generation, I find, never adapt properly because their boredom threshold is so alarmingly low.

At the risk of sounding a crotchetty old man, I believe the players of today cannot handle having a lot of time on their hands. Their restlessness is reflected in their cricket. They are so used to the hectic action of one-day cricket that the long, almost meditative spells which any Test match contains simply bore them. Touring patterns off the field have changed, too. Players do not talk about cricket of their own volition these days. They will discuss it very lucidly in a formal meeting, and they might reflect on the past day's play over an evening beer, but they have no interest in talking about other facets of the game, which I think is a pity. Indeed, rather than sitting around the team-room with a few cans of beer and a lot of cricket chat, the modern trend is for the young player to shut himself off underneath stereo headphones, or close his mind to anything but the video screen. These forms of entertainment hold little appeal to me. I sat through a few films in Pakistan, when I felt too ill to move any further and when the choice, in Faisalabad, was strictly limited anyway; but my general view is that there must be more to life than such solitary time-filling.

I would, however, be the first to admit how lonely touring can become. There are literally hours on end with nothing apparently to do – especially in eastern civilizations such as Pakistan. For a player who cannot get in the side, for reasons of form or injury, and finds himself faced with days and maybe weeks of net practice and nothing else, the whole experience can become one of abject misery and home can seem millions rather than thousands of miles away. With this in mind, I would also criticize the trendy reluctance to attend social functions. While agreeing that some are stuffy to an unfriendly degree, these receptions are laid on largely by people with the team's welfare in mind and, in most countries, by British expatriates whose hospitality is welcoming and convivial. If you don't go to these functions, where do you meet people? The hotel bar? Now here we come on to another contentious subject.

It would seem from our experiences on this tour that the so-called popular press now consider international cricketers to be fair game for their attentions. Just like politicians and pop stars, it appears our private lives are no longer our own. This may at first glance appear a trifling inconvenience to bear as the price of stardom – after all, think of all those social climbers who attend London's trendiest spots night after night just longing to be pictured in compromising positions by one of the gossip columns. Cricketers in general, however, have no pretensions to social climbing and I, for one, find the media's growing obsession with smut and sensation deplorable.

We suffered from it in New Zealand and Pakistan, but there are plenty of other examples to point to. I came home to read that the phone of John Francome, champion jockey, had been tapped for two months and that the *Daily Mirror* were threatening to publish the tapes. How can that be defended? The newspaper editor claimed it was in the interests of the public, but I tended to agree with the High Court judge who, in granting Francome an injunction, gave his view that certain newspapers nowadays confuse the interests of the public with the interests of their own circulation figures.

It is this grubby circulation war which has prompted every newspaper – to one degree or another – to mimic the methods of the top-selling paper, *The Sun*. My own first experience of modern, unscrupulous journalism came in 1977, shortly after I had turned down an offer from Kerry Packer to join World Series Cricket. I was in Northumberland, conveniently remote from pressmen, and I had deliberately revealed nothing of my reasons for declining Packer's offer. Imagine my surprise, therefore, when I heard the Birmingham *Evening Mail* had run a story quoting me at length on why I turned down a fortune to stay loyal to England. The quotes had simply been invented and, although the journalist concerned left the paper immediately, the instances of invention are plainly still on the increase as newspapers use whatever means are at their disposal, and plenty which should not be, to boost their sales that vital bit more.

We first heard of the media interest in our off-field activities quite early on during the New Zealand leg of the tour. There was the farcical episode with Mr Brooks and the *Daily Express* – the businessman's complaints about drunkenness receiving page one treatment but the subsequent explanation of mistaken identity being ignored. Then, much more sinister, we heard that at least one New Zealand journalist was trying to justify an allegation that certain of our players had been smoking pot in the dressing-room during our Christchurch Test defeat. Alan Smith and I went through the motions of discussing it, but the whole thing was really too preposterous to cause us any loss of sleep. Anyone with the slightest knowledge of cricket grounds would know that people wander in and out of dressing-rooms all the time, rendering the thought of surreptitious pot-smoking laughable, even if anyone was that way inclined.

But still the rumours grew, culminating in a series of front-page stories published by English papers while we were in Pakistan. As I write, the possibility of a court case prevents me commenting in any detail on the allegations, but I will say that ever since I have been in the game, tours have involved a certain amount of drinking and a certain amount of female hangers-on. Nothing has changed. The proudest boast of one prominent ex-England player is that one day on an Australian tour just after the war, he drank twenty-seven beers without having a pee. If he had done that on this year's tour, he would probably have found himself on the front pages.

Where things have altered is that players tend to do their drinking in the hotel bars rather than in the team-room. They have more money than they used to, and some of them enjoy spending it in a sociable environment. Less beer is drunk these days, and rather more wine and spirits, but in general I fancy there are fewer heavy drinkers around than there used to be.

The trouble with being seen in the hotel bars most nights is that gossip starts all to easily. Perhaps some players have a naive faith in the press. Ian Botham has fallen into this trap, believing that anything he may say in a bar is off the record. Just because he would never let a mate down, he thinks everyone else is made that way. It is irresponsible, I am afraid, because the job of the journalist is to criticize when the team is playing badly and there are many players who feel let down when a writer they had been sharing a drink with the previous night lets fly in print about his inadequacies. So long as those criticisms are confined to playing performances, I do not think the player has much cause to complain – the journalist is simply doing what he is paid for. But when the copy contains some fairly poisonous allegations about his social behaviour, we are into an entirely different situation and one which, I fear, may radically alter the life of cricketers on tour.

In the light of what happened during this tour, I can envisage future squads being very much more confined, in the style of soccer players. It could be a case of travelling everywhere together by bus, spending all free time in the team-room and being banned from drinking in the hotel bar. It would be a sorry end to what has always been a very special cameraderie, but if players' private lives are to be so closely scrutinized it may be the job of the cricket authorities to ensure they are largely invisible.

The basic problem is that, whatever the subjects of newspaper stories may know to be true, it is human nature for people to believe what they read – not only that but, in most cases, positively to gloat over it. The average man or woman, with a totally unglamorous job, likes nothing better than seeing the weaknesses of public figures exposed. Be they film stars, pop stars or sportsmen, any inference that they are homosexual/drunkards/unfaithful/drug-takers is apparently lapped up with relish. After the events of this tour, the press-player relationship in cricket has been severely damaged, and I honestly don't know how the pieces can be picked up.

There were other social issues recurring on this tour which had nothing to do with the press. Wives were one. Now that inter-national cricketers are comparatively well paid, most can afford to bring out their wives or girlfriends on tour whenever they wish, and for how long they wish. Hard-and-fast rules are very difficult to apply. The stipulation used to be that wives could come out for a set three-week period, but some players argued that this was not long enough. There are some players whose cricket improves for having their wife around, but there are others who find themselves under an extra, unwanted pressure. If the wife/girlfriend has sat around the pool getting bored while her husband has been playing all day, it is understandable that she might want to go out somewhere lively in the evening. But all the player wants to do is soak in the bath, eat in the coffee-shop and go to bed. Touring, as I have said, is an unnatural existence and not all wives can be expected to adapt and understand the pressures.

The tour might have had more than its fair share of problems, but I do feel there were areas in which the planning was proved to be sensible. Our decisions to dispense with a second wicket-keeper and to take only two spinners instead of three were undoubtedly correct – the itinerary would have made the extra players quite redundant. I feel the balance of the side was as good as it could have been in the light of having only one all-rounder, in Botham, and a non-batting wicket-keeper; and I would defend all our selections. The best players were chosen yet it was undoubtedly one of the weakest England sides ever to go abroad.

I do not believe Mike Brearley would have produced different results. I do not think any captain could have improved the side very much. But I do accept some of the criticism of my captaincy. It is, for instance, always very difficult to keep proper control over the side while bowling, especially off a long run-up such as mine. I admit I found that hard, and I certainly leaned heavily on my senior players for help while I was bowling.

The popular criticism that we were captained 'by committee' and that I allowed too many others to become involved in field-setting is understandable though rather misleading. The help offered to me by the likes of Botham, Gower and Taylor, especially when I was bowling but also if I was not at the right angle to assess a particular fielder's position, has been interpreted as undermining my authority. It can look bad if two or three players are simultaneously waving their arms to adjust the field. It is not ideal. But my own view is that it is better to get things right that way than to assume a dictatorial control which simply ignores mistakes.

My handling of Ian Botham has also not been well received. At Christchurch I was taken to task for allowing him too long a spell. But we had only four bowlers in the side – two had to bowl into the wind for long periods and one of these, Tony Pigott, was a Test rookie. Botham simply had to bowl.

It is said I let him bowl to ridiculously attacking fields. That, on occasions, has been true, but Ian's mental make-up is such that if he can't bowl to the type of aggressive field-setting which turns him on, he is unlikely to perform at all. Sadly, his bowling has steadily declined in quality since 1981. I fear his interest in cricket has also waned. The loss of the England captaincy left a scar on him and his relationship with what he calls Lord's and what I call the Test and County Cricket Board has been slightly antagonistic ever since. Having said that, I do not accept that his stature as a world-class cricketer is necessarily diminishing and he certainly contributed more to this tour, on and off the field, than he did in Australia twelve months earlier.

There were some other bright spots on the tour, notably the advances made by our young seam bowlers, Neil Foster and Norman Cowans. Both did enough to suggest they have a decent future at Test level, but I can't help feeling they were forced into the side two years too soon when the South African bans suddenly robbed us of John Lever, Chris Old and Mike Hendrick. It should only be now, in 1984, that Foster and Cowans are pushing established bowlers for their places, but circumstances dictated that we had hardly any established bowlers left.

Graham Dilley also worked far harder than he has been given credit for in some quarters and it is a tragedy for him and for England that he will miss all the 1984 season through injury. Bob Taylor's consistency is too often taken for granted and the efforts of Nick Cook and Vic Marks, two workmanlike cricketers who would have been unlikely to play Test cricket in a richer playing age, were worthy of praise.

If I stop there and start struggling for inspiration, it may be because I am a natural pessimist. But I believe the reason for our mediocre Test side is buried within the structure of our county game, and that things are unlikely to improve unless changes are made. I have spent a lot of time and energy trying to convince people that the answer lies in playing four-day Championship cricket midweek, with two limited-overs competitions at weekends to draw the crowds. But I find I am getting nowhere. In general, Test players are in favour of my ideas, but the vast majority of county players know they will never play for England and cannot see why they should play a longer and potentially less exciting form of Championship cricket just to benefit the international players.

County officials raise local objections which, to my mind, are shortsighted. They claim they would lose revenue from member-ship and gate receipts if the current structure was altered, and that they would then be at risk of bankruptcy. While certainly not mock-ing the financial predicament of counties, it is surely a fact that they are kept afloat not by gate money, or even subscriptions – but by their split of the Test match receipts. Taking that a stage further, I said two years ago that cricket could follow soccer in the sense that a poor national team will steadily lose the support of the public – and hence the counties will find their cut of the cash diminishing. There are arguments on both sides, I will concede, but surely experiment is worthwhile.

My own future was undeniably clouded when I arrived home prematurely, not least because my debilitating illness left me with precious little energy to give it much immediate thought. Through a combination of poor results and media pressure I was plainly no longer secure as England captain: indeed, I faced a fight for fitness in order to regain my place in the team.

Looking back over the two years since that unexpected phone call from Peter May telling me I was the new skipper, there have ob-viously been good times and bad, some fulfillment and a certain amount of frustration, largely brought on by the confines of my authority. When I came back from Australia last year, for instance, I asked if I could have the six or eight best fast-bowling prospects in England up at Edgbaston for a week of special coaching and training pre-season, because I considered we had lost the Ashes through a shortage of fire-power. My request was thought impractical because, at that stage, the selectors had not reappointed me.

There is a case for a full-time manager to organize such things, but perhaps his job, too, would hang on the thin thread of results. All of sport is alike – just count the number of soccer managers who come to grief each season. Once failure gets a grip, the tide of popular opinion, inevitably swelled by press comment, is for changes at the top. But I am not bitter. Whatever happens in my career, at least I have captained England.

ENGLAND TEST AVERAGES

Batting

Batting	NEW ZEALAND Wellington	Christchurch	Auckland	R	Av	PAKISTAN Karachi	Faisalabad	Lahore	R	Av	COMBINED R	Av
D. I. Gower	33	2 8	26 —	69	17.25	58 57	152 —	9 173*	449	112.25	518	64.75
D. W. Randall	164	0 25	104 —	293	73.25	8 16	65 —	14 0	103	20.60	396	44.00
I. T. Botham	138	18 0	70 —	226	56.50	22 10	—	—	32	16.00	258	43.00
C. L. Smith	27 30*	—	91 —	148	74.00	28 5	66 —	18 15	132	26.40	280	40.00
V. J. Marks	—	—	6 —	6	6.00	5 1	83 —	74 55	218	43.60	224	37.33
M. W. Gatting	19 —	19* —	0 —	38	19.00	26 4	75 —	0 53	158	31.60	196	28.00
G. Fowler	—	4 10	0 —	14	4.67	—	57 —	58 19	134	44.67	148	24.67
C. J. Tavaré	9 36*	3 6	—	54	18.00	—	—	—	—	—	54	18.00
A. J. Lamb	13 —	11 9	49 —	82	20.50	20 —	19 —	29 6	78	15.60	160	17.77
N. A. Foster	10 —	—	18* —	28	28.00	1* 0*	—	6 0	6	3.00	34	11.33
N. G. Cowans	—	4 7	21 —	32	10.67	—	—	6 —	7	7.00	39	9.75
R. W. Taylor	14 —	2 15	23 —	54	13.50	4 19	0 —	3* 3	29	5.80	83	9.22
N. G. B. Cook	7 —	—	—	7	7.00	9 5	1* —	1 5	18	6.00	25	6.25
R. G. D. Willis	5* —	5 0	3 —	14	4.67	6 2	—	—	8	4.00	22	4.40

Bowling

Bowling	NEW ZEALAND Wellington	Christchurch	Auckland	O	M	R	W	Av	PAKISTAN Karachi	Faisalabad	Lahore	O	M	R	W	Av	COMBINED O	M	R	W	Av
R. G. D. Willis	3/37	4/51	3/109 0/7	115.1	28	306	12	25.50	2/33 0/13	—	2/89 5/42	19	6	46	2	23.00	134.1	34	352	14	25.14
N. G. Cowans	—	3/52	2/98 0/4	52	14	154	5	30.80	0/34 0/10	—	1/117 0/73	57.3	11	175	7	25.00	109.3	25	329	12	27.42
N. G. B. Cook	1/43 3/153	—	1/78	89.3	37	196	4	49.00	6/65 5/18	—	5/67 0/44	178.3	54	444	14	31.71	268	91	640	18	35.56
N. A. Foster	1/60 2/91	—	1/70	91	29	229	4	57.25	2/90	2/133 0/38	1/109 1/10	82	20	230	7	32.86	173	49	459	11	41.72
I. T. Botham	—	—	0/70	109.4	25	354	7	50.57	—	—	—	30	5	90	2	45.00	139.4	30	444	9	49.33
V. J. Marks	5/59 1/137	1/88	3/115	40.2	9	115	3	38.33	0/40 1/23	1/59 1/26	1/59 0/53	90	24	260	4	65.00	130.2	33	375	7	53.57

Played in one match A. C. S. Pigott (2nd Test v NZ) 4, 8*, 17-7-75-2 and G. R. Dilley (2nd Test v P) 2*, 37-6-142-5.

Also bowled M. W. Gatting 15-4-64-2, C. L. Smith 5-2-8-1 and G. Fowler 1-0-3-0.

Catches 12 Taylor; 8 Gatting; 7 Botham; 5 Gower, Lamb; 4 Cowans†; 3 Smith; 2 Foster, Fowler†, Randall; 1 Cook, Tavaré, Willis.

† includes one as substitute.